Talk Time

Everyday English Conversation

Teacher's Book 1

Susan Stempleski

Genevieve Kocienda

OXFORD

UNIVERSITY PRESS

OXFORD
UNIVERSITY PRESS

198 Madison Avenue
New York, NY 10016 USA

Great Clarendon Street, Oxford OX2 6DP UK

Oxford University Press is a department of the University of Oxford.
It furthers the University's objective of excellence in research, scholarship,
and education by publishing worldwide in

Oxford   New York

Auckland Cape Town Dar es Salaam Hong Kong Karachi
Kuala Lumpur Madrid Melbourne Mexico City Nairobi
New Delhi Shanghai Taipei Toronto

With offices in

Argentina Austria Brazil Chile Czech Republic France Greece
Guatemala Hungary Italy Japan Poland Portugal Singapore
South Korea Switzerland Thailand Turkey Ukraine Vietnam

OXFORD and OXFORD ENGLISH are registered trademarks of
Oxford University Press.

Market Development Director, Asia: Chris Balderston
Senior Editor: Patricia O'Neill
Art Director: Maj-Britt Hagsted
Senior Designer: Stacy Merlin
Designer: Sangeeta E. Ramcharan
Art Editor: Elizabeth Blomster
Production Manager: Shanta Persaud
Production Coordinator: Soniya Kulkarni

ISBN: 978 0 19 438204 5

Printed in Hong Kong.

10 9 8 7 6 5 4 3 2

ACKNOWLEDGMENTS

Illustrations by: Kathy Baxendale pp.98,102; Mark Collins pp.93,100; William
Waitzman pp.91,92.

*We would like to thank the following for their permission to reproduce the photograph on
the cover:* Corbis.

Photocopiable activities written by: Lewis Lansford.

The publishers would like to thank the following for their help in developing this series:
Mei-ho Chiu, Taiwan; Kirsten Duckett, Seoul, South Korea; Laura MacGregor,
Tokyo, Japan; Grant Warfield, Seoul, South Korea; Andrew Zitzmann, Osaka,
Japan.

*The publishers would also like to thank the following OUP staff for his support and
assistance:* Ted Yoshioka.

Contents

Scope and sequence _____

Unit	Theme	Grammar	Vocabulary
1 page 1	Meeting people Countries and nationalities	*To be*; subject pronouns, possessive adjectives; Yes/No questions and short answers	Name, address, telephone number; country, nationality
2 page 8	Family Describing people	*Wh-* questions; *have*	Family relationships; adjectives: height, weight, age
3 page 15	In a classroom In an electronics store	*This / that*; preposition *on*; *these / those*; plurals	Classroom objects: book, pen, pencil; small electronics: MP3 player, laptop, cell phone
4 page 22	Everyday activities Places	Present continuous: statements, Yes/No questions; *Wh-* questions; preposition *at*	Daily activities: studying, eating, sleeping; locations and places
5 page 29	Foods and drinks Snacks	Simple present; agreeing and disagreeing; count and noncount nouns; *How much / How many*	Food and drink, meals, restaurant vocabulary; snack foods, *a lot*
6 page 35	Housing In an apartment	*There is / there are*; prepositions of place	House, apartment, rooms; furniture
7 page 41	Free-time activities Popular sports	Information questions; adverbs of frequency; *can* for ability	Leisure activities; sports, exercise, hobbies
8 page 47	Life events Weekend plans	*Be going to* future; *Wh-* questions	Life events; special occasions; weekend activities
9 page 53	Movies TV programs	*Wh-* questions; adverbs of frequency	Types of movies; types of TV programs
10 page 59	Health problems Getting better	*Feel* + adjective; *have* + noun; imperatives	Ailments, illnesses, and health; remedies
11 page 65	On vacation Past events	Simple past: questions and statements; *to be*: simple past	Vacation locations and activities; life events in the past; time markers
12 page 71	Telephone language Things to do	Requests with *can* and *could*; object pronouns; *would*; verb + *to*	Telephone language; taking and leaving messages; chores

To the teacher _____

Welcome to *Talk Time: Everyday English Conversation*, a three-level series for high-beginning to low-intermediate students of American English. As the title suggests, the course stresses speaking and listening skills. It is especially suitable for learners who have already studied some English, but who may still lack the confidence and skills to effectively participate in conversation in real-life situations. I hope that this Teacher's Book will help making teaching with *Talk Time* more effective and enjoyable.

The primary goal of *Talk Time* is to help learners develop fluency in spoken English. The course is based on a syllabus that combines essential vocabulary and the basic grammatical features of English with fun and relevant topics that motivate learners and encourage them to express their personal ideas, feelings, and opinions.

All three levels of *Talk Time* feature systematic presentation of vocabulary, task-based listening activities, essential grammar points, model conversations in a wide variety of settings, and interactive activities that maximize students' speaking time. The books also include optional activities for additional speaking practice.

Course length

Each level of *Talk Time* provides between 24 and 36 hours of classroom instruction. For classes that have more instruction time available, the Teacher's Book offers suggestions for optional Extension activities. In classes where less time is available, teachers can reduce the amount of time spent on the Grammar activities.

Components

Each level of Talk Time consists of a Student Book with an accompanying Student CD, a Teacher's Book, a Class CD, and a Test Booklet with CD.

Student Book

The Student Book contains 12 thematic units, each divided into 2 lessons. The lessons focus on high-interest, everyday topics such as meeting people, free-time activities, and shopping. Each lesson contains various sections, including Speaking, Listening, Grammar, and Conversation. These four sections introduce the vocabulary and grammar students will practice in the unit. Each lesson ends with a Communication task that enables students to practice the language of the lesson in a communicative activity, often in the form of an information gap, survey, or role play.

Check your English contains a one-page review for each unit at the back of the book. It provides written practice, and it reviews grammar and vocabulary from each unit. There is also a unit-by-unit list of Key vocabulary at the back of the Student Book.

• Student CD

The Student CD is included at the back of the Student Book and contains recordings of all of the dialogues in the Conversation sections of the Student Book. Students can use the CD to practice the dialogues and do extra listening practice outside the class.

- **Teacher's Book**

  The Teacher's Book features step-by-step instructions for each unit, including warm-up and review activities, as well as audio scripts for all the material recorded on the Class CD and Student CD, answer keys to exercises, and notes about cultural and linguistic points. The Teacher's Book also suggests optional extension activities that enable you to adapt lessons to different classroom situations.

  In addition, the Teacher's Book contains 24 optional activities at the back of the book. These photocopiable activity sheets can be used as a warm-up, a review, or simply to break up the routine of the classroom and get students "out of the book."

- **Class CD**

  The Class CD features audio renditions of the Speaking, Listening, Grammar, and Conversation sections. The audio program provides many opportunities to listen to native and non-native speakers of English in a variety of listening activities.

  1. *Speaking.* This section provides pronunciation models of the vocabulary items.

  2. *Listening.* The task-based listening activities present the vocabulary of the lesson in context and encourage students to focus on the new vocabulary.

  3. *Grammar.* The text in the grammar paradigms is provided as a model for students.

  4. *Conversation.* In this section, the vocabulary and grammar of the lesson are presented in a larger context. Students listen to the dialogue and also have the opportunity to practice the language.

- **Test Booklet with CD**

  The Test Booklet with CD contains a photocopiable test for each unit, as well as an answer key and complete audio script. The booklet is accompanied by its own audio CD that contains recordings for all of the listening sections of the tests.

Unit organization

The Student Book contains 12 units, each divided into 2 lessons. Each lesson is a self-contained series of activities focusing on a main topic with related vocabulary and grammar. Interactive activities, mostly in the form of pair work, are presented in each lesson. Each lesson follows the same basic structure. The systematic presentation of relevant vocabulary at the beginning of each lesson helps to prepare students for the speaking and listening activities that follow. The interactive task, which is at the end of each lesson, enables students to review, extend, and personalize the language they practiced earlier in the lesson.

Lesson structure

Each lesson contains the following five sections, always in the same sequence: Speaking, Listening, Grammar, Conversation, and Communication task.

- **Speaking**

  Each lesson begins with a Speaking section that introduces and illustrates key vocabulary related to the topic. Students listen to new words and expressions and then practice using them with a partner. The speaking activities are designed to focus students' attention on the new vocabulary items and provide personalized practice using the new words and expressions. In most cases, these speaking activities require pairs of students to practice short dialogues.

- ### Listening

  The Listening section presents the new vocabulary in context. Students listen to short dialogues and do task-based listening activities. To make it easier for students to do the activities while they listen, writing is kept to a minimum. Students are asked to write single words or short phrases, or to choose correct answers by checking, circling, or numbering items.

- ### Grammar

  Each Grammar section contains a summary of an essential grammar point. In addition to presenting a summary of a key grammar point, the second lesson of each unit provides personalized practice in the form of pair work.

- ### Conversation

  The Conversation section presents the grammar and vocabulary of the lesson within the larger context of a conversation. Students listen and then practice the conversation with a partner. Finally, they practice the conversation again, substituting their own information.

- ### Communication task

  The final section of each lesson is a Communication task that consolidates and builds on the language of the lesson and provides an opportunity for students to speak more freely about the topic. These interactive activities usually take the form of pair or group work; sometimes they involve the whole class. They may be self-contained on one page, or they may be presented on two pages, with a part for Student B to look at in the back of the book. To sustain student interest and motivation, various types of interactive activities are offered, such as games, information-sharing, and role playing.

  Each lesson may also contain one or more of the following:

- ### Memo

  Brief notes that remind students about the rules of English and help them complete an activity

- ### Extra

  A short activity that moves beyond the book and provides students with additional speaking practice

- ### Helpful language

  A short list of sample questions or phrases to help students perform an activity and keep on talking

  At the back of the book are 12 Check your English pages, along with a unit-by-unit list of the Key vocabulary used in the text. The Check your English pages review the vocabulary and grammar presented in each unit. These pages can be done by students working individually, in pairs, or as a class. They can also be assigned for homework, or they may be used as tests to evaluate students' progress at the end of each unit. An answer key for each page is located in the Teacher's Book.

General guidelines for teaching with *Talk Time*

The five sections of each lesson in *Talk Time* are linked. For example, the vocabulary introduced and practiced in the Speaking section is put into context in the Listening section. The language point in the Grammar section and the vocabulary of the lesson are presented in the context of a dialogue in the Conversation section. The activities in the earlier sections of the lesson—Speaking, Listening, Grammar, and Conversation—prepare students for the freer Conversation task that ends the lesson.

Teaching vocabulary

Vocabulary is a major element and the starting point of each lesson in *Talk Time*. Each Speaking section introduces an average of 8–12 vocabulary items related to the topic.

Each new vocabulary item is illustrated, and the whole list is recorded on the Class CD. When teaching new vocabulary, the following guidelines may be helpful:

- When introducing new vocabulary, focus students' attention on the pictures of vocabulary items as well as on the written forms of the words.

- Before having students repeat the items in a vocabulary list, allow them to listen to how the items are pronounced on the recording. Postpone repetition exercises until students have had a chance to listen to all of the items once or several times.

- Pronunciation can be especially problematic for learners of English because there is often no clear relation between how a word is written and how it is pronounced. Train students to listen to exactly how new vocabulary words are pronounced. Provide opportunities for students to listen to vocabulary while looking only at the illustrations. (Students can cover the written forms of the words with their hands, a bookmark, or a piece of paper.)

- Identify and repeat words that you think will cause pronunciation problems for your students. Highlight stress patterns by tapping them on a table or desk.

- Use checking questions to ensure that students understand the meaning of individual vocabulary items.

- Point out any items that follow irregular or unpredictable grammar patterns, for example, noncount nouns or words followed by a particular preposition.

In cases where it is necessary to use additional means to get across the meaning of a vocabulary item, the following techniques may be helpful:

- Use mime. The technique of acting out meanings works particularly well with action verbs. It also makes things more memorable and can be fun.

- Provide simple English-language definitions. Use words students already know to get new meanings across. If necessary, use a learner dictionary to locate appropriately clear and simple definitions.

- If you know the students' first language, translation can be a fast and efficient way to get a meaning across. Keep in mind that not every word has a direct translation.

- Think of a clear context in which the vocabulary item is used, and describe it to the students.

• Give students example sentences in which the word is used.

The technique you choose will depend on the individual vocabulary item. Some techniques are more suitable for particular words. A combination of techniques can often be helpful and memorable.

Teaching listening skills

Listening is one the most difficult skills for many learners of English. The Listening sections in *Talk Time* are designed to help students make regular and effective progress in understanding conversational English. Sometimes the activities in the Listening section act as an extension of the vocabulary-based activities in the Speaking section, or as an introduction to the structural point outlined in the Grammar section.

The Listening section in the first lesson of each unit presents a single activity in which students usually have to listen to a recording and identify key vocabulary. The second lesson of each unit presents two listening activities, both based on the same recording. Activity A requires students to listen and identify the situation, context, or topic. Activity B requires them to listen again and understand details of the listening text. When teaching listening, the following guidelines may be helpful:

• Have students do prelistening activities to prepare them for listening tasks. Prelistening activities include asking and answering questions about the topic, discussing the pictures (if available), and making predictions about what students will hear on the recording.

• Remind students that in most listening situations, the goal is to understand the main idea or information. Point out that they usually don't have to understand everything on the recording and encourage them to focus on main ideas first.

• Before playing the recording, make sure that students understand what they have to do to complete the listening task.

• Where necessary or appropriate, play the recording more than once.

• Have students work together in pairs or groups to check answers to listening tasks.

• After students have completed a listening activity and checked their answers, play the recording again. Many students will appreciate a second chance to confirm or identify correct answers.

Teaching grammar

Appropriate use of grammar is essential to effective speaking. When teaching grammar, the most important thing to remember is that learners do not become proficient in grammar by only studying and/or memorizing grammar rules. People become proficient in grammar by using the language in situations in which particular grammar is necessary. When teaching grammar, keep the following strategies in mind:

• Use the Class CD to present the examples in the grammar boxes.

• When necessary, offer additional examples to illustrate particular grammar points.

- Use the examples in the grammar boxes as a speaking drill. Pause after each example on the recording, and allow individuals or the whole class to repeat the example sentence.

- To check students' comprehension of individual grammar points, ask students to provide example sentences of their own.

- Where appropriate, model how to do the first item in the related grammar task.

- Have students work in pairs or groups to compare answers to grammar tasks.

- To check students' answers and provide feedback, elicit answers to grammar tasks from volunteers around the class.

Teaching speaking skills

Many different kinds of activities in *Talk Time* focus on speaking skills: sample dialogues, conversations, and communication tasks in the form of pair work, group work, or whole class activities.

Sample dialogues

Each Speaking section includes two speaking activities. The first (A) is a short sample dialogue for students to practice with a partner. The second (B) is a more personalized speaking activity in which pairs of students exchange their own ideas and information. These short speaking activities help to build confidence and maximize speaking practice in class. For students who are unfamiliar with pair work, it may be useful to remind them that practicing with a partner helps to improve their English by giving them more opportunities to speak and listen to English in class.

Conversations

Each Conversation section in *Talk Time* has a model conversation that includes the key grammar and vocabulary of the lesson. Each model conversation has two activities: A and B. Activity A is a controlled activity in which students listen to the conversation and then practice it with a partner. Activity B is freer and more personalized. Students use the conversation as a model, but they vary the language using their own information.

Encourage students to speak and listen as naturally as possible when practicing conversations. They should try to maintain eye contact with their partner when listening or speaking. Teach them to use the "read and look up" technique. Students first read a line of dialogue to themselves, then look up and make eye contact with their partner as they speak the line aloud. As students practice a conversation, circulate among them and encourage them to maintain eye contact throughout the conversation.

Because the conversations present the key language of the lesson, accurate repetition is important, especially when doing Activity A. When students practice the conversations, be sure to have them switch roles, so that they get additional listening and speaking practice. After students have practiced a conversation a few times, pairs of students can be asked to act it out for the class.

In some cases, the Conversation sections include an Extra speaking activity. These activities provide additional opportunities for personalized speaking practice related to the model conversation. Whether you have students do an Extra speaking activity will depend on your class's needs and the time available.

Communication tasks

The Communication tasks in *Talk Time* include a wide variety of activity types, such as games, picture differences, role plays, surveys, and "talk about" activities. They are usually designed for pairs or small groups of students, but in a few cases they may involve the whole class working together. In every case, they are designed to engage the students in fluency-oriented language work that is interesting, useful, and fun.

When doing communication activities, try to keep the following suggestions in mind:

- Organize pairs or groups so that learners of different ability levels work together. Mixed-ability groupings will encourage students to help and learn from one another.

- Unless specified otherwise, limit groups to no more than three or four students. This will encourage more participation and increase talking time per student.

- Vary pair and group arrangements so that students do not always work with the same classmates.

- Encourage students to use as much English as possible.

- As students carry out a speaking activity, walk around the class and discretely monitor them as they work. Notice any difficulties they seem to be having with vocabulary, grammar, or pronunciation. You may then choose to provide immediate feedback to individuals, pairs, or groups. Alternatively, you may prefer to take notes and share your observations with the whole class later on.

- When giving feedback, be sure to focus on one point at a time. Giving too much information at one time can overwhelm learners.

- When students are practicing dialogues, encourage them to use the "read and look up" technique in which they maintain eye contact while listening or speaking to a partner. Remind students that clarity and natural-sounding language are more important than speed. Encourage them to dramatize the dialogues through the use of appropriate body language.

I have enjoyed writing *Talk Time*. I hope you enjoy teaching the course, and that the exercises and activities in the book motivate your students and help them become better and more confident speakers of English. I have made every effort to make the course useful, interesting, and enjoyable for both you and your students. I invite you to send me any comments about the course that you or your students would like to share with me.

Sincerely,

Susan Stempleski

To the student

Welcome to *Talk Time*. Let's take a look at a unit.

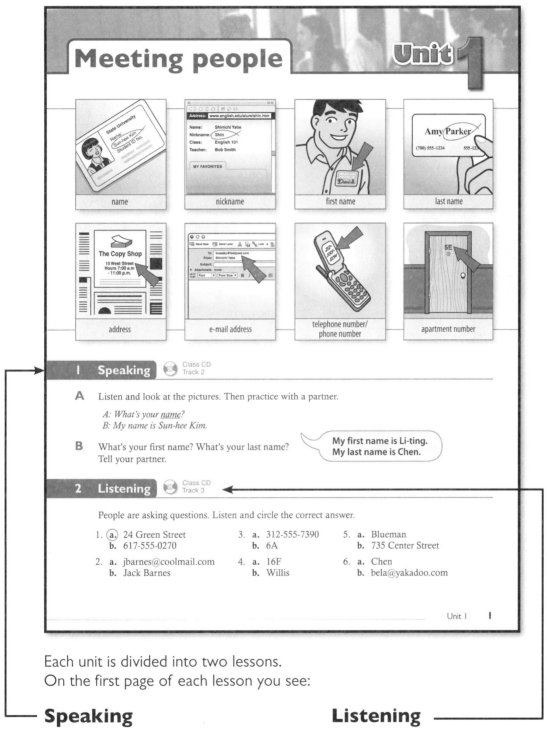

Each unit is divided into two lessons.
On the first page of each lesson you see:

Speaking

First you practice the new vocabulary for this lesson. You will listen to the CD, and look at the pictures. Then you practice using the new words with a classmate.

Listening

In this section, you listen to the vocabulary in short conversations and answer some questions.

On the second page of each lesson you see:

Grammar

In this section, you see the grammar focus for this lesson. You listen to the CD, and then practice the grammar.

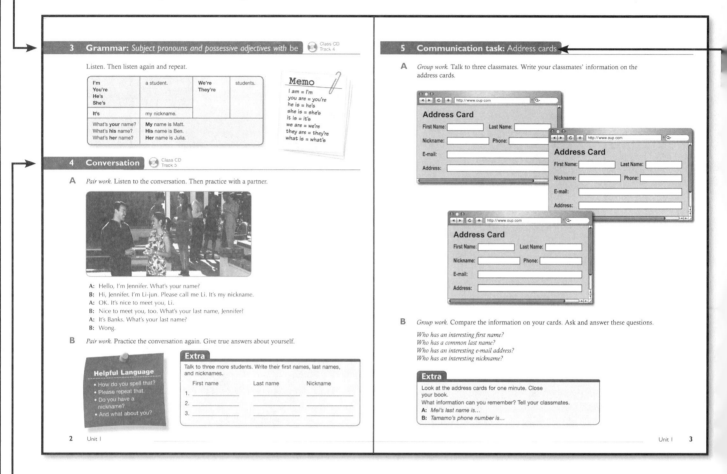

Conversation

In this section, you listen to a conversation and then practice with a partner. This lets you practice the vocabulary and grammar of the lesson in a larger context. It also lets you use your own information.

On the third page of each lesson you see:

Communication task

In this section, you practice the language of the lesson with a partner or a small group. This section lets you use your own information to speak more freely about the topic. Sometimes you and your partner will look at the same page, and sometimes you will look at different pages.

Other things you see in the unit:

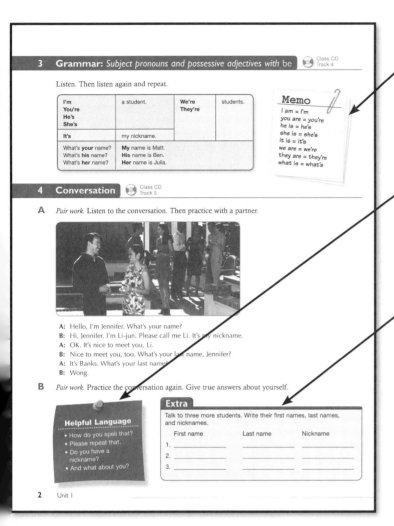

Memo

The *Memo* reminds you about rules of English that are different from your language, for example, contractions. The language in the Memo will help you complete the activities.

Helpful Language

The Helpful Language note gives you questions or phrases that will help you complete the activities. They provide cues you can use to keep talking longer with your partner.

Extra

Sometimes you will see an Extra activity. This lets you practice more with the same language from the activity.

CD icon

The CD icon tells you that this activity is recorded on the audio CD, and your teacher may play it in class in order for you to do the activity.

Check your English

At the back of the book, there is a review page called *Check your English*. This page gives you a chance to review the language from the unit.

Every lesson gives you time to listen to English and time to talk with your classmates. *Talk Time* will help you increase your vocabulary and improve grammatical accuracy. I hope you enjoy studying with *Talk Time*. Good luck!

Meeting people

Components

Student Book: pages 1–6

Check your English: page 77

Class CD: tracks 2–9

Student CD: tracks 2 and 3

Target language

Vocabulary: Personal information: *name*, *address*, *telephone number*; country; nationality

Grammar: *To be*; subject pronouns; possessive adjectives; Yes/No questions and short answers

Themes: Meeting and greeting people; countries and nationalities

---

Student Book page 1

Warm-up

Point to yourself and say *I'm (Pat)*. Point to a student and have them say *I'm (Ken)*. Continue around the class with all the students.

1 Speaking

Class CD, Track 2

Presentation

1. Focus students' attention on the pictures and the text below each one. Explain that they will hear the terms on the CD.

2. Focus students' attention on the pictures again. Have students describe what they see.

Activity A

1. Have students read the directions for the activity.

2. Focus students' attention on the pictures and the text below them. Play Class CD Track 2. Have students listen and look at the pictures. Have students repeat. Go over any words they don't know.

    #### Audio script

    name   nickname   first name   last name

    address   e-mail address

    telephone number / phone number   apartment number

3. Explain to students that they will take turns asking and answering questions about the pictures.

4. Model the conversation with a student volunteer.

5. *Pair work.* Put students in pairs and have them do the activity.

6. Ask students questions about the pictures to check understanding.

Notes

1. Explain to students that a first name is the name their parents gave them when they were born, a last name is their family name, and a nickname is a name that friends or family use for someone.

2. Explain to students that a nickname can be a shortened or different version of someone's name, such as *Jon* for *Jonathan*, *Meg* for *Margaret*, or *Chuck* for *Charles*. A nickname can also refer to someone's physical appearance or abilities, such as *Red* for someone with red hair, or *Speedy* for someone who can run fast. Ask students if they have a nickname.

3. You may want to tell students that some of these terms differ in the United Kingdom and the United States. For example, *first name* is used in the U.S., but *given name* is common in the U.K. *Last name* is used in the U.S., but *surname* is more common in the U.K.

4. Explain to students that an address has a house or apartment building number and apartment number followed by a street name.

Activity B

1. Have students read the directions for the activity.

2. Explain to students that they will take turns asking and telling a partner their first and last name.

3. *Pair work.* Focus students' attention on the speech bubble. Have students do the activity.

4. Have students tell the class their partner's first and last name.

2 Listening

Class CD, Track 3

1. Have students read the directions for the activity.

2. Explain to students that they will listen to people ask questions about personal information and circle the correct answer. Have students read the answer

choices. Answer any questions about vocabulary.

3. Play the first question on Class CD Track 3. Make sure everyone understands why the correct answer is *a*. Play the rest of the recording. Have students do the activity. Play the recording again if necessary.

Audio script

1. What's your address?
2. What's your name?
3. What's your phone number?
4. What's your apartment number?
5. What's your nickname?
6. What's your e-mail address?

4. Ask volunteers to read their answers for the class to check.

Answers:

1. **a.** 24 Green Street
2. **b.** Jack Barnes
3. **a.** 312-555-7390
4. **a.** 16F
5. **a.** Blueman
6. **b.** bela@yakadoo.com

Notes

You might want to explain to students how e-mail addresses are usually read in English. For example, the address in **2a** is read as *j barnes at coolmail dot com*, and the address in **6b** is read as *bela at yakadoo dot com*.

Student Book page 2

3 Grammar: Subject pronouns and possesive adjectives with *be*

Class CD, Track 4

1. Have students read the directions for the activity.

2. Have students look at the grammar box. Give them time to read the examples.

3. Make sure students understand that a pronoun is a word that can be substituted for another noun. Explain to students that subject pronouns are the subject in a sentence and possessive adjectives tell *whose*.

4. Focus students' attention on the **Memo**. Read the information about contractions with students and answer any questions.

5. Play Class CD Track 4. Have students listen. Play the recording again and have students repeat.

Audio script

A: I'm a student.
B: You're a student.
A: He's a student.
B: She's a student.
A: It's my nickname.
B: We're students.
A: They're students.

A: What's your name?
B: My name is Matt.
A: What's his name?
B: His name is Ben.
A: What's her name?
B: Her name is Julia.

6. Say a sentence using specific nouns (*That's Kim. Kim is a student.*). Have a student volunteer say the sentences again with pronouns (*Her name is Kim. She's a student.*). Continue with other sentences and different students.

7. Ask various students each of the questions in the grammar box to check understanding.

Notes

Explain to students that the contracted form is normally used in conversation. Encourage students to use contractions, as this will help to make their speech more fluent.

4 Conversation

Class CD, Track 5

Activity A

1. Focus students' attention on the photo. Ask them to say where they think the people are, what they're doing, or what they're saying to each other.

2. Have students read the directions for the activity.

3. Play Class CD Track 5 or read the conversation twice.

Audio script

A: Hello. I'm Jennifer. What's your name?
B: Hi, Jennifer. I'm Li-jun. Please call me Li. It's my nickname.
A: OK. It's nice to meet you, Li.
B: Nice to meet you, too. What's your last name, Jennifer?
A: It's Banks. What's your last name?
B: Wong.

4. *Pair work.* Have students read the conversation, switching roles.

5. Ask several pairs to demonstrate for the class.

Also on Student CD, Track 2

Notes

Explain that *Hi* is an informal way to say *Hello.* Point out that *It's nice to meet you* and *Nice to meet you* mean the same thing. Explain that these phrases are said the first time we meet someone, not with people we already know.

Activity B

1. Have students read the directions for the activity. Explain that they will work with a partner and take turns saying each part in the conversation from Activity A. This time they will substitute true information about themselves.

2. *Pair work.* Have students do the activity.

3. Ask several pairs to demonstrate for the class.

Extra

1. Have students read the directions for the activity.

2. Explain to students that they will talk to three classmates and take turns asking about their first name, last name, and nickname. Tell students to write the information in the chart.

3. Focus students' attention on the **Helpful Language** note. Review the questions with the class by brainstorming when to use these questions and some appropriate answers.

4. Model the activity with a student to be sure the students understand what to do.

5. Have students do the activity.

Extension

Have students think of nicknames for everyone in the class.

Student Book page 3

5 Communication task:
Address cards

Activity A

1. Have students read the directions for the activity.

2. Focus students' attention on the address cards. Ask students to say what information they will fill out. To help put the activity in context, ask students if they have an on-line address book for their friends and family. Point out that this information is similar to the information in many e-mail address books.

3. Explain to students that they will talk to three classmates and fill out the address cards with true information. (If students are concerned about giving out this information, tell them that they can make something up.)

4. To check understanding, ask student volunteers what question they will ask to get each piece of information. Write the questions on the board for students' reference (or refer them to the **Helpful Language** note on page 2) if necessary.

5. *Group work.* Have students do the activity.

Activity B

1. Have students read the directions for the activity.

2. Focus students' attention on the list of questions. To check understanding, ask students what is the most interesting name they have heard, and what is the most common name in their country.

3. Model the activity with a student volunteer.

4. *Group work.* Put students in new groups and have students compare the information on their cards and answer the questions.

5. Have several groups tell the class their answers.

Extra

1. Have students read the directions for the activity and the examples.

2. Have students look at their completed address cards for one minute. Then have students close their books.

3. Ask students what information they can remember about their classmates.

Extension

Discuss the following questions as a class or in small groups:

Do you like your first name? If not, what would you like it to be?

Explain your nickname. If you don't have a nickname, what do you think your nickname should be?

Do you think it's good to give a child an unusual name?

Countries and nationalities

Warm-up and review

Put students in pairs and have them practice introducing themselves to each other. Put a sample dialogue on the board as a guide if necessary.

6 Speaking

Class CD, Track 6

Presentation

Focus students' attention on the flags and the country names and nationalities below each one. Explain that they will hear the terms on the CD.

Activity A

1. Have students read the directions for the activity.

2. Focus students' attention on the flags and text below them. Play Class CD Track 6. Have students listen and look at the pictures. Have students repeat. Go over any words they don't know.

Audio script

Australia, Australian	Brazil, Brazilian
China, Chinese	India, Indian
Japan, Japanese	Korea, Korean
the U.K., British	the U.S., American

3. Explain to students that they will take turns asking and answering questions using the pictures as cues.

4. Model the sample conversation with a student volunteer.

5. *Pair work.* Put students in pairs and have them do the activity.

6. Ask students questions about the flags to check understanding.

Notes

Explain that *U.S.* stands for *United States* and *U.K.* stands for *United Kingdom*. Point out to students that these two country names are always preceded by *the*.

Activity B

1. Have students read the directions for the activity.

2. Explain to students that they will now ask their partner their nationality. If you are in a monolingual class, tell students that they can pretend to be from another country for variety of answers.

3. *Pair work.* Focus students' attention on the speech bubble. Have students do the activity.

4. Have students tell the class their partner's nationality.

7 Listening

Class CD, Track 7

Activity A

1. Have students read the directions for the activity.

2. Explain to students that they will listen to people introduce themselves and ask about nationality. Explain that they will listen to the conversations and choose the correct answer for the question, *Who's meeting who?*

3. Play the first conversation on Class CD Track 7. Make sure everyone understands why the correct answer is *c*. Have students do the activity. Play the recording again if necessary.

Audio script

1.

A: Hello. I'm Xian. What's your name?

B: My name's Paul. It's nice to meet you, Xian. Where are you from?

A: I'm from China. And what about you, Paul? Where are you from?

B: I'm from Australia.

2.

A: Hi, My name's Amelia.

B: Nice to meet you, Amelia. My name's David. Where are you from?

A: I'm from the U.S. And you? Where are you from?

B: I'm from the U.K.

3.

A: Hi, there! I'm Nelson.

B: Oh, hi, Nelson. I'm Devi.

A: Devi. Where are you from?

B: India. And where are you from?

A: I'm from Brazil.

4. Ask volunteers to read their answers for the class to check.

Answers:

1. **c**, Xian met Paul
2. **a**, Amelia met David
3. **b**, Nelson met Devi

Notes

Explain that *What about you?* and *And you?* are common ways to ask someone the same question that they have just asked you. *Hi, there* is an informal, friendly way to say *hello*.

Activity B

1. Have students read the directions for the activity.

2. Explain to students that they will listen to the CD again and fill in the blanks in the name tags with each speaker's country.

3. Play the first conversation again. Make sure everyone understands why the correct answer is 1. *China*, c. *Australia*. Play the rest of the recording again. Have students do the activity.

4. Ask volunteers to read their answers for the class to check.

Answers:

1. Xian, from China	a. David, from the U.K.
2. Amelia, from the U.S.	b. Devi, from India
3. Nelson, from Brazil	c. Paul, from Australia

Student Book page 5

8 Grammar: Yes/No questions and short answers with *be*

Class CD, Track 8

Activity A

1. Have students read the directions for the activity.

2. Have students look at the grammar box. Give them time to read the examples.

3. Focus students' attention on the **Memo**. Read the information with students and answer any questions about the contracted forms.

4. Play Class CD Track 8. Have students listen. Play the recording again and have students repeat.

Audio script

A: Are you Korean?

B: Yes, I am.

C: No, I'm not.

A: Is he Indian?

B: Yes, he is.

C: No, he isn't.

A: Are you Brazilian?

B: Yes, we are.

C: No, we aren't.

A: Are they American?

B: Yes, they are.

C: No, they aren't.

5. Ask various students each of the Yes/No questions in the grammar box to check understanding. Nod or shake your head to elicit an affirmative or negative answer.

Notes

1. You might want to point out to students that the final /t/ sound in contractions is not always articulated in American English.

2. Explain that the intonation of Yes/No questions rises at the end.

Activity B

1. Have students read the directions for the activity. Point to each flag and ask student volunteers which country it belongs to. (Refer students to page 4 if necessary.)

2. *Pair work.* Have students take turns asking and answering questions about the nationality of the person or people in each photo. Model a conversation with a student volunteer if necessary. Encourage students to ask questions that will elicit both affirmative and negative responses.

3. Have several pairs say one of the conversations for the class.

Answers:

Hongan Li: He's Chinese.
Maya Patel: She's Indian.
Simon Baker: He's British.
Mi-young Choi: She's Korean.
Nicki Watts: She's Australian.
Sumio Ito: He's Japanese.
Mateus Diaz: He's Brazilian.
Jan and Mike Smith: They're American.

Notes

Explain to students that the short answers *Yes, I am.* / *Yes, he is.*, etc., cannot be contracted to: *Yes, I'm.* / *Yes, he's.*, etc.

9 Conversation

Class CD, Track 9

Activity A

1. Focus students' attention on the picture. Ask them to say where they think the people are and what they're doing.

2. Have students read the directions for the activity.

3. Play Class CD Track 9 or read the conversation twice.

   ### Audio script

   A: Hi, are you in this class?

   B: Yes, I am.

   A: What's your name?

   B: My name's Gina.

   A: Nice to meet you. I'm Steve. Where are you from, Gina?

   B: I'm from Brazil. How about you? Are you British?

   A: No, I'm not. I'm Australian.

4. *Pair work.* Have students read the conversation, switching roles.

5. Ask several pairs to demonstrate for the class.

   Also on Student CD, Track 3

Activity B

1. Have students read the directions for the activity. Explain that they will work with a partner and take turns saying each part in the conversation from Activity A. This time they will substitute true information about themselves.

2. *Pair work.* Have students do the activity.

3. Ask several pairs to demonstrate for the class.

Student Book page 6

10 Communication task:
Who's in the news?

Activity A

1. Have students read the directions for the activity.

2. Focus students' attention on the pictures. Have students identify what is happening in each one.

3. Focus students' attention on the phrase under each picture. Point to each and model pronunciation. Have students repeat. To check understanding, have students name one person for each category.

4. Explain to students that they will think of famous business people, movie stars, athletes, etc., who have been in the news lately. Then they will write the name of each person under the corresponding picture.

5. Have students complete the activity on their own.

Activity B

1. Have students read the directions for the activity.

2. Focus students' attention on the pictures of the man and the passport. Ask students to say what they think the man's job is (e.g., *a business person, politician*, etc.), and where he's from (e.g., *he's American/from the U.S.*).

3. Focus students' attention on the sample conversation. Model it with a student volunteer.

4. Focus students' attention on the scorecard. To check understanding, ask students what they will use it for (to write a point for each fact they know about each person).

5. Explain to students that they will work with a partner and take turns saying what they know about each person and marking their scorecards.

6. *Pair work.* Have students do the activity.

Extension

1. Have students say who they chose for each category and what they know about that person. Have other people in the class add more information if they can.

2. Conduct a class poll on:

   Who knew the most information about the people in general?

   Who knew the most information about one person?

   Who was the most common person that people in the class chose?

   Who thought of the most unusual people for each category?

3. Have students do Activity B again. This time have students choose one student in the class to talk about. If students do not know each other, have each stand up and say some facts about themselves. Let students take notes.

Check your English

To review the vocabulary and grammar from Unit 1, have students do page 77. This page can be done individually, in pairs, or as a class. It can also be assigned for homework. Alternatively, administer this page as a test at the end of the unit.

Answers:

A Vocabulary
1. phone number
2. address
3. India
4. name
5. apartment
6. e-mail address
7. Japanese
8. nationality

B Grammar
1. **d.** It's nice to meet you, too.
2. **a.** James Bond.
3. **b.** Brazil.
4. **e.** No, he isn't. He's British.
5. **c.** Yes, they are.
6. **g.** Nice to meet you, Nelson.
7. **f.** Yes, I am.

Family

Components

Student Book: pages 7–12

Check your English: page 78

Class CD: tracks 10–17

Student CD: tracks 4 and 5

Target language

Vocabulary: Family relationships; adjectives: height, weight, age

Grammar: *Wh-* questions; *have*

Themes: Family; describing people

Student Book page 7

Warm-up and review

1. Divide the class into pairs. Give students a few minutes to create a simple dialogue using the language and theme from Unit 1.

2. Have pairs practice their dialogues. Circulate and help as needed.

3. Ask a few pairs to say their dialogue for the class.

1 Speaking

Class CD, Track 10

Presentation

1. Focus students' attention on the pictures and the list of family terms. Explain that they will hear the terms on the CD.

2. Focus students' attention on the pictures again. Have students describe what they see.

Activity A

1. Have students read the directions for the activity.

2. Focus students' attention on the pictures and the numbered list of family terms next to them. Play Class CD Track 10. Have students listen and look at the pictures. Have students repeat. Go over any words they don't know.

Audio script

1. husband	10. grandmother
2. wife	11. grandson
3. father	12. granddaughter
4. mother	13. uncle
5. son	14. aunt
6. daughter	15. nephew
7. brother	16. niece
8. sister	17. cousin
9. grandfather	

3. Have students look at the pictures and go over the names of the people as a class.

4. Explain to students that they will take turns asking and answering questions about the people in the pictures.

5. Model the sample conversation with a student volunteer.

6. *Pair work.* Put students in pairs and have them do the activity.

7. Ask students questions about the pictures to check understanding.

Notes

Explain to students that in English-speaking countries, there are no separate terms for older and younger siblings, and that *cousin* is a gender-neutral term.

Activity B

1. Have students read the directions for the activity.

2. Explain to students that they will look at the pictures and talk about Nina's family with their partner.

3. Focus students' attention on the **Memo**. Read the information with students and answer any questions.

4. *Pair work.* Focus students' attention on the speech bubble. Have students do the activity.

5. Have volunteers talk about Nina's family so students can check their answers.

2 Listening

Class CD, Track 11

Presentation

1. Have students read the directions for the activity.

2. Explain to students that they will listen to people talk about their families and circle the answer to the question, *Who are they talking about?* Read the answer choices aloud with the class.

3. Play the first conversation on Class CD Track 11. Make sure everyone understands why the correct answer is *b*. Play the rest of the recording. Have students do the activity. Play the recording again if necessary.

Audio script

1.

A: Wow! You have a lot photos!

B: Yeah. This is a photo of my brother and me.

A: What's your brother's name?

B: Gary.

2.

A: That's me with my daughter and son.

B: Oh, they're cute! What are their names?

A: My son's name is Ryan, and my daughter's name is Kelley.

3.

A: This is my father and mother with my aunt.

B: Which one is your mother?

A: The one on the right.

4.

A: That's my grandmother and that's my grandfather.

B: And who are the children?

A: They're my cousins!

5.

A: And who's in this photo? Are they your cousins?

B: No, that's a photo of my aunt and uncle.

A: Wow. They're young.

B: Yeah, they are.

6.

A: Who's this?

B: Oh, that's my sister.

A: Do you have brothers?

B: No, just one sister.

4. Ask volunteers to read their answers for the class to check.

Answers:

1. **a.** brother
2. **b.** children
3. **a.** parents and aunt
4. **b.** grandparents and cousins
5. **a.** aunt and uncle
6. **a.** sister

Notes

Explain to students that *Yeah* is an informal way to say *Yes*, and *Wow* is an informal interjection used to express that you are surprised by something.

Student Book page 8

3 Grammar:
Wh- questions with *be*

Class CD, Track 12

1. Have students read the directions for the activity.

2. Have students look at the grammar box. Give them time to read the examples.

3. Focus students' attention on the **Memo**. Read the information with students and answer any questions.

4. Play Class CD Track 12. Have students listen. Play the recording again and have students repeat.

Audio script

A: What's your name?

B: My name is Ken.

A: Where are you from?

B: I'm from New York.

A: How are you?

B: I'm fine.

A: Who's that?

B: That's my sister.

A: How old is she?

B: She's 16.

A: Who are they?

B: They're my parents.

5. Assign different students in the class to be various family members of each other. Ask various students each of the questions in the grammar box to check understanding.

Notes

Explain that the intonation of *Wh-* questions goes down at the end.

4 Conversation

Class CD, Track 13

Activity A

1. Focus students' attention on the picture. Ask them to say where they think the people are and what they are doing.

2. Have students read the directions for the activity.

3. Focus students' attention on the **Memo**. Read the information with students and answer any questions.

4. Play Class CD Track 13 or read the conversation twice.

Audio script

A: Nice pictures. Hey, who's that?
B: That's my brother.
A: What's his name?
B: His name is Sung-ho.
A: How old is he?
B: He's 26.
A: Is he married?
B: No, he isn't. He's single.

5. *Pair work.* Have students read the conversation, switching roles.

6. Ask several pairs to demonstrate for the class.

   Also on Student CD, Track 4

Notes

You may want to explain that *Hey* is an informal interjection. It has several meanings, and in this case, it's used to express interest on the part of the speaker. When said in a different tone of voice, however, it can be considered impolite.

Activity B

1. Have students read the directions for the activity. Explain that they will work with a partner and take turns to practice the conversation using their own information. Make sure they understand that they should give true answers.

2. Give students time to draw a picture of a family member. Alternatively, students can use photos of family that they may have with them in class.

3. *Pair work.* Have students do the activity.

4. Ask several pairs to demonstrate for the class.

Extra

1. Keep partners in pairs and have them read the directions for the activity and the example.

2. *Pair work.* Have students do the activity.

3. Have students tell the class about their partner's picture.

Student Book page 9

5 Communication task:
My family tree

Activity A

1. Have students read the directions for the activity. Make sure they understand the meaning of *family tree*.

2. Focus students' attention on the sample family tree. To check understanding, ask students, *Where would you write your name? Where would you write your mother's name? Where would you write your grandmother's name? If you have brothers or sisters, where would they be in the family tree?*

3. Have students draw their family tree.

Notes

1. Explain to students that in the U.S. and Canada, there is usually a distinction made between a nuclear family and an extended family. Tell them that a nuclear family consists of mother, father, and children; and an extended family consists of grandparents, aunts, uncles, etc.

2. Explain to students that in the U.S. and Canada, it's uncommon for an extended family to live together in the same house. In fact, it's quite common for extended family members to live very far away from each other and only see each other a few times a year.

Activity B

1. Have students read the directions for the activity.

2. Focus students' attention on the **Helpful Language** note. Review the questions by brainstorming appropriate answers with the class.

3. *Pair work.* Have students do the activity.

4. Have several pairs tell the class about their partner's family tree.

Notes

1. Teach students other family terms that might be useful: *in-law* (the family of your spouse), *sibling* (a gender-neutral term for brother or sister), and *only child* (used for someone who has no brothers and sisters).

2. Remind students that with Yes/No questions there is rising intonation.

Extension

1. Talk about how English does not have highly defined terms for family relations. For example, the second daughter of my younger brother is called *niece* and the third daughter of my older brother is also called *niece*. Discuss with students if family terms are more specific in their language.

2. Tell students that *mom* and *dad* are informal for *mother* and *father*. *Grandpa* and *grandma* are often used instead of *grandfather* and *grandmother*. Discuss with students the various names for *mother, father, grandmother,* and *grandfather* in their language.

3. Divide the class into groups of three or four. Have one student describe their family tree, or a made-up one. The other students in the groups draw the family tree. Have them check their trees with each other to see if they look the same. Have each student take a turn describing a family.

Describing people

Warm-up and review

Divide the class into pairs. Give students three or four minutes to find out as much as they can about each other's families. Then have volunteers tell the class about their partner's family.

6 Speaking

Class CD, Track 14

Presentation

1. Focus students' attention on the four pictures and the text below each one. Explain that they will hear the terms on the CD.

2. Explain that height, weight, hair color, and age can be used to describe a person.

3. Make sure students understand the vocabulary: To show the relationship between *tall, average height,* and *short,* draw simple stick figures on the board illustrating each height. Do the same for weight. Draw a chart with *young, old,* and *middle-aged* on the board and ask students to help you fill it out with appropriate ages. For *good-looking, handsome, pretty, beautiful,* and *cute,* elicit famous celebrities that can be described by each adjective.

Notes

1. Point out to students that they must be careful when describing someone's weight. In the U.S., it is a sensitive issue. If someone is not fat at all, it is polite to say they are *slender* or *slim. Skinny* implies that they are too thin and can be an insult. If a person is fat or heavy, it is best not to say anything at all about their weight.

2. Explain that age can also be a sensitive issue and that it is best not to ask anyone's age unless you know them very well.

3. Explain that *cute* is used to describe adults as well as children.

Activity A

1. Have students read the directions for the activity.

2. Focus students' attention on the pictures and the text below them. Play Class CD Track 14. Have students

listen and look at the pictures. Have students repeat. Go over any words they don't know.

Audio script

Height:	tall	average height	average height	short
Weight:	thin	average weight	average weight	heavy

Hair:	short, curly, blond	short, straight, dark
	long, straight, dark	long, straight, blond

Age:	in his twenties	old	middle-aged	young

Other:	good-looking/handsome	pretty/beautiful
	cute	

3. Explain to students that they will take turns asking and answering questions about the people in the pictures.

4. Model the sample conversation with a student volunteer.

5. *Pair work.* Have students do the activity.

6. Ask students questions about the pictures to check understanding.

Activity B

1. Have students read the directions for the activity.

2. Explain to students that they will now describe themselves to their partner.

3. *Pair work.* Focus students' attention on the speech bubble. Have students do the activity.

4. Have student volunteers describe themselves for the class.

Notes

Make sure students do not become confused with the two common meanings of *like* (*similar* and *to enjoy*). The question *What are you like?* is a common way to ask someone to describe their physical appearance or personality. Explain that they will have to listen closely to the context to know which meaning is being used.

7 Listening

Class CD, Track 15

Activity A

1. Have students read the directions for the activity.

2. Explain to students that they will listen to people describe someone and check what the speaker says. Make sure students understand they will only check the first two columns: **Hair** and **Height**.

3. Play the first conversation on Class CD Track 15. Make sure students understand why the correct answers are *Hair: dark* and *Height: average height*. Play the rest of the recording. Have students do the activity. Play the recording again if necessary.

Audio script

1.

A Tell me about your brother, Jill.

B: Well, his name's Jack. He has dark hair. He's very cute.

A: Oh… Is he tall?

B: No. He's average height.

2.

A: Tell me about your son, Betsy.

B: Well, his name's Kenny. He's tall and his hair is very long.

A: How old is he?

B: He's 25.

3.

A: Is your cousin good-looking, Bob?

B: Oh, yeah. She's blond and she's very pretty.

A: Is she tall?

B: Yes, she is.

4.

A: What's your sister like, Miki?

B: Her hair is dark brown, and she's not very tall. She's very good-looking.

A: Hmm. Is she single?

B: No. She's married.

Answers:

Checked items are as follows.

	Hair	Height
1.	dark	average height
2.	long	tall
3.	blond	tall
4.	dark	short

4. Ask volunteers to read their answers for the class to check.

Activity B

1. Have students read the directions for the activity.

2. Explain to students that they will listen to the CD again and check who the speaker is talking about. Make sure students understand they will check only one person in the last column, **Relationship**.

3. Play the first conversation on Class CD Track 15 again. Make sure everyone understands why the correct answer is *brother*. Play the rest of the recording again. Have students do the activity.

4. Ask volunteers to read their answers for the class to check.

Answers:

Checked items are as follows.

Relationship

1. brother
2. son
3. cousin
4. sister

Student Book page 11

8 Grammar: Using *have*

Class CD, Track 16

Activity A

1. Have students read the directions for the activity.

2. Have students look at the grammar box. Give them time to read the examples.

3. Focus students' attention on the **Memo**. Read the information with students and answer any questions.

4. Play Class CD Track 16. Have students listen. Play the recording again and have students repeat.

Audio script

A: I have straight hair. I don't have curly hair.

B: She has blue eyes. She doesn't have brown eyes.

A: Do you have short hair?

B: Yes, I do.

C: No, I don't

A: Does she have long hair?

B: Yes, she does.

C: No, she doesn't.

5. Ask various students each of the questions in the grammar box to check understanding.

Point out that English speakers rarely use the uncontracted form (*No, I do not,* or *No, he does not*) in Yes/No answers. Have them practice saying the negative answers, making sure they pronounce the final /t/ sound.

Activity B

1. Have students read the directions for the activity. Focus students' attention on the speech bubble. Answer any questions about vocabulary.

2. *Pair work.* Have students take turns making sentences that describe themselves.

3. Have students tell the class how their partners described themselves.

9 Conversation

Class CD, Track 17

Activity A

1. Focus students' attention on the photo. Ask them to say where they think the women are and what the women are talking about.

2. Have students read the directions for the activity.

3. Play Class CD Track 17 or read the conversation twice.

   Audio script

   A: So, tell me about Dan. Is he good-looking?
   B: Oh, yes. He's handsome.
   A: Is he tall?
   B: No, he isn't tall. He's average height.
   A: Does he have blue eyes?
   B: No, he doesn't. He has brown eyes and dark hair.
   A: Does he have long hair?
   B: No, he doesn't. His hair is short and curly.

4. *Pair work.* Have students read the conversation, switching roles.

5. Ask several pairs to demonstrate for the class.
   Also on Student CD, Track 5

Activity B

1. Have students read the directions for the activity. Explain that they will work with a partner and take turns to practice the conversation using their own information. Make sure they understand that they should give true answers.

2. *Pair work.* Have students do the activity.

3. Ask several pairs to demonstrate for the class. Alternatively, have student volunteers tell the class about their partner's friend or family member.

Student Book page 12

10 Communication task:
Who am I?

1. Have students read the directions for the activity.

2. Focus students' attention on the sample conversation and the picture. To check understanding, ask students, *Why are the students posing? What are the people thinking?* (For example, *He's thinking of an athlete who won a medal. She's thinking of an actress going to an award ceremony, a premiere,* etc.)

3. Demonstrate the task. Think of a famous person and elicit questions from students. If necessary, brainstorm possible questions first. Make sure students understand that the questions should all elicit Yes/No answers or one-word answers.

4. *Group work.* Have students do the activity.

Notes

Brainstorm other vocabulary that can be used in the game such as occupations (*actor, baseball player,* etc.) or adjectives (*single, intelligent, talented, fast, funny,* etc.). Write the words on the board for students' reference.

Extra

1. Have students read the directions for the activity.

2. Focus students' attention on the sample conversation. Make sure students understand they will ask questions with Yes/No answers or one-word answers.

3. Give students time to think of a famous person.

4. *Group work.* Have partners take turns asking and answering questions about the person.

5. Have students tell the class who they chose and describe him/her.

Extension

Bring in pictures of very different-looking people from magazines. Tape them to the board and number them. Have students take turns describing the people and have the class guess who the student is describing.

Check your English

To review the vocabulary and grammar from Unit 2, have students do page 78. This page can be done individually, in pairs, or as a class. It can also be assigned for homework. Alternatively, administer this page as a test at the end of the unit.

Answers:

A Vocabulary
1. young
2. son
3. handsome
4. uncle
5. short
6. middle-aged
7. husband
8. average height

B Grammar
1. <u>Where</u> is she from?
2. <u>How old</u> is he?
3. <u>Who</u> are they?
4. <u>Does</u> he have dark hair?
5. <u>How</u> are you?
6. <u>Who's / Who is</u> that?
7. <u>Do</u> you have a sister?
8. <u>Is</u> she married?

In a classroom

Components

Student Book, pages 13–18; 73

Check your English: page 79

Class CD, tracks 18–26

Student CD, tracks 6 and 7

Target language

Vocabulary: Classroom objects: *book, pen, pencil*; small electronics: *MP3 player, laptop, cell phone*

Grammar: *This, that*; preposition *on*; *these, those*; plurals

Themes: In a classroom; In an electronics store

Student Book page 13

Warm-up and review

1. Divide the class into groups of five or six. Have one student (S1) say one or two sentences about his/her family (*I have three older sisters. They have dark hair.*).

2. Have the next student (S2) say one or two sentences about his/her family and repeat the information about S1's family.

3. Have students continue around the group until the last student repeats all the information about the other students' families.

1   Speaking

Class CD, Track 18

Presentation

1. Focus students' attention on the picture and the numbered list of classroom vocabulary next to it. Explain that they will hear the terms on the CD.

2. Focus students' attention on the picture again. Have students describe what they see. Ask them what things they can see in their own classroom right now.

Notes

Make sure students hear the difference between *a* + noun and *an* + noun.

Activity A

1. Have students read the directions for the activity.

2. Focus students' attention on the picture and the numbered list of classroom vocabulary next to it. Play Class CD Track 18. Have students listen and

look at the picture. Have students repeat. Go over any words they don't know.

Audio script

1.	a clock	10.	a notebook
2.	a wall	11.	a desk
3.	a bulletin board	12.	a chair
4.	a board	13.	a floor
5.	an eraser	14.	a wastebasket
6.	a ruler	15.	a book
7.	an electronic dictionary	16.	a table
8.	a pencil	17.	a bookbag
9.	a pen	18.	a map

3. Focus students' attention on the **Memo**. Read the information with students and answer any questions.

4. Explain to students that they will take turns asking and answering questions about the items in the picture.

5. Model the sample conversation with a student volunteer.

6. *Pair work.* Have students do the activity.

7. Ask students questions about the picture to check understanding.

Activity B

1. Have students read the directions for the activity.

2. Explain to students that they will look at the picture and the list of words and talk with their partner about which classroom objects they have.

3. *Pair work.* Focus students' attention on the speech bubbles. Have students do the activity.

4. Have students talk about what their partner has so the class can check their answers.

2 Listening

Class CD, Track 19

1. Have students read the directions for the activity.

2. Focus students' attention on the photos at the bottom of the page. Elicit the name of each item.

3. Explain to students that they will listen to people ask about classroom objects and number the pictures in the order they hear them.

4. Play the first question on Class CD Track 19. Make sure everyone understands why item **c** is numbered *1*. Play the rest of the recording. Have students do the activity. Play the recording again if necessary.

Audio script

1. Who has my pencil?
2. Is that your electronic dictionary?
3. Where's my book?
4. Do you have an eraser?
5. Is this your ruler?
6. Do you know where my notebook is?

5. Ask volunteers to read their answers for the class to check.

Answers:

a. 5   b. 4   c. 1   d. 6   e. 2   f. 3

Student Book page 14

3 Grammar: *This/that*; preposition *on*

Class CD, Track 20

1. Have students read the directions for the activity.

2. Have students look at the pictures. Give them time to read the sentences above each picture.

3. Focus students' attention on the **Memo**. Read the information with students and answer any questions.

4. Play Class CD Track 20. Have students listen. Play the recording again and have students repeat.

Audio script

A: This is a book. It's on the desk.
B: This is a notebook. It's on the table.
A: That's a clock. It's on the wall.
B: That's a wastebasket. It's on the floor.

5. Place different classroom objects around the classroom. Make sure some of them are close to students.

6. To check understanding, point to an object and have a student say a sentence about it using *this* or *that*. Continue around the class with all the objects.

4 Conversation

Class CD, Track 21

Activity A

1. Focus students' attention on the photo. Ask them to say where they think the people are, what they're doing, or what they're saying to each other.

2. Have students read the directions for the activity.

3. Play Class CD Track 21 or read the conversation twice.

Audio script

A: Is this your pen, Vicki?
B: No, it isn't. Ask Tim.
A: Tim?
C: Yeah?
A: Is this your pen?
C: Yes, it is. Thanks a lot!
A: No problem. And … is this your notebook?
C: Hmm. No, it's not. Where's your notebook, Vicki?
B: On my desk … Oh, no, it isn't. That's my notebook!

4. *Group work.* Have students read the conversation, switching roles three times so each student reads each part.

5. Ask several groups to demonstrate for the class.

Also on Student CD, Track 6

Notes

Remind students that *Yeah* is an informal way to say *Yes*. Explain that *Thanks a lot* is an informal way to say *Thank you very much. No problem* is an informal way to say *You're welcome.*

Activity B

1. Have students read the directions for the activity. Explain that they will work with two partners and take turns to practice the conversation using their own information. This time they will substitute their own names and objects into the conversation.

2. *Group work.* Have students do the activity.

3. Ask several groups to demonstrate for the class.

Extra

1. Put students in pairs and have them read the directions for the activity and the examples.

2. Have partners do the activity. Brainstorm other classroom vocabulary if necessary.

3. Have students tell the class about objects in the classroom.

Student Book page 15

5 Communication task: I Spy

Class CD, Track 22

Presentation

1. Focus students' attention on the **Memo**. Read the information with students and answer any questions.

2. Explain that I Spy is a popular game in the U.S.

Activity A

1. Have students read the directions for the activity.

2. Focus students' attention on the alphabet. Play Class CD Track 22. Have students listen and repeat, or review the alphabet as a class.

Audio script

A B C D E F G H I J K L M N O P Q R
S T U V W X Y Z

3. Point to the letters in random order and have student volunteers say them. Pick up speed as you do the activity.

Activity B

1. Focus students' attention on the photo. Ask them to say where they think the people are and what they're doing.

2. Have students read the directions for the activity. To check understanding, demonstrate the activity with a student volunteer using the sample conversation as a guide.

3. *Group work.* Have students in each group take turns thinking of an object and guessing the object. Play to a time limit.

Notes

1. Remind students that the answer *Yes, it is* cannot be contracted to *Yes, it's.*

2. Remind students that with Yes/No questions there is rising intonation.

Extra

1. Put students in pairs or small groups and have them read the directions for the activity.

2. Have students do the activity.

3. Have students tell the class what page they picked and which objects they guessed.

Extension

1. Have students make a simple drawing of a room in their house. Put them in small groups and have them take turns using their pictures to play I Spy.

2. Have students work in pairs and think of one classroom object for as many letters as they can. Play to a time limit. The pair with the most correct objects wins.

In an electronics store

Student Book page 16

Warm-up and review

Divide the class into pairs. Give students three or four minutes to find out what objects students have in their bookbags. Have volunteers tell the class about their partner's bookbags.

6 Speaking

Class CD, Track 23

Presentation

1. Focus students' attention on the picture of electronics and the numbered list of vocabulary. Explain that they will hear the terms on the CD.

2. Focus students' attention on the picture again. Have students describe what they see.

Activity A

1. Have students read the directions for the activity.

2. Focus students' attention on the picture and the numbered list of vocabulary next to it. Play Class CD Track 23. Have students listen and look at the picture. Have students repeat. Go over any words they don't know.

   #### Audio script

1. a laptop	8. a speaker
2. an MP3 player	9. a cell phone
3. a television / a TV	10. a camcorder
4. a camera	11. a boom box
5. a digital camera	12. a DVD player
6. headphones	13. a video game system
7. a karaoke machine	14. a CD player

3. Explain to students that they will take turns asking and answering questions about the items in the picture.

4. Model the sample conversation with a student volunteer.

5. *Pair work.* Have students do the activity.

6. Ask students questions about the picture to check understanding.

Notes

1. Make sure students understand that the article *a/an* is used for singular objects. However, even though *headphones* is a singular object, it is made of a pair of objects. Therefore, it does not take the singular article.

2. Explain to students that a *cell phone* is also called a *mobile* or *mobile phone*, although these terms are more common in British English.

Extension

1. Have students use their dictionaries to look up the words *lap* and *boom*. Then have them say how these words relate to the words *laptop* and *boom box*.

2. Ask students if any of the vocabulary items are in the classroom right now. Ask students which items play music/games/movies, which ones can be used to write a letter/take a picture/make a movie. Have students explain the difference between a camera and a digital camera, and an MP3 player and a CD player.

Activity B

1. Have students read the directions for the activity.

2. Explain to students that they will look at the picture and the list of words and talk about which electronics they have and don't have with their partner.

3. *Pair work.* Focus students' attention on the speech bubble. Have students do the activity.

4. Have student volunteers talk about what their partner has so the class can check their answers.

7 Listening

Class CD, Track 24

Activity A

1. Have students read the directions for the activity.

2. Focus students' attention on the photos at the bottom of the page. Elicit the name of each item.

3. Explain to students that they will listen to people talk about items in an electronics store and number the pictures in the order they hear them.

4. Play the first speaker on Class CD Track 24. Make sure everyone understands why item **c** is numbered *1*.

Play the rest of the recording. Have students do the activity. Play the recording again if necessary.

Audio script

1. This is a nice camera. It's easy to use, and it takes good pictures.
2. Uh, I don't like this laptop very much. It's very heavy, and the screen is too small.
3. Wow! Look at that boom box. It's really small. But listen to that sound. It's great!
4. This DVD player is kind of expensive, and it isn't very good. And the screen is too small.
5. Isn't this a fabulous MP3 player? I like it because it's so small.

5. Ask volunteers to read their answers for the class to check.

> **Answers:**
>
> a. 3   b. 5   c. 1   d. 2   e. 4

Activity B

1. Have students read the directions for the activity.

2. Explain to students that they will listen to the CD again and check the correct answer for the question, *Do the people like the items?* Read the answer choices and make sure students understand what to do.

3. Play the first speaker on Class CD Track 24 again. Make sure everyone understands why the correct answer for **c** is *Likes it*. Play the rest of the recording again and have students do the activity.

4. Ask volunteers to read their answers for the class to check.

> **Answers:**
>
> a. Likes it   d. Doesn't like it
> b. Likes it   e. Doesn't like it
> c. Likes it

Student Book page 17

8 Grammar: *These/those*; plurals

Class CD, Track 25

Activity A

1. Have students read the directions for the activity.

2. Have students look at the pictures. Give them time to read the questions and answers above the pictures.

3. Focus students' attention on the **Memo**. Read the information with students and answer any questions.

4. Play Class CD Track 25. Have students listen. Play the recording again and have students repeat.

Audio script

A: These are clocks.

A: What are these?

B: They're cell phones.

A: Those are books.

A: What are those?

B: They're cameras.

5. Place pairs of different classroom objects around the classroom. Make sure some of them are close to students.

6. To check understanding, point to a pair of objects and have a student volunteer say a sentence about them using *these* or *those*. Continue around the class with all the objects.

7. Repeat the activity with single items and pairs of items together so students can review *this* and *that*.

Notes

Remind students that the intonation of *Wh-* questions goes down at the end.

Activity B

1. Have students read the directions for the activity. Focus students' attention on the sample answers. Ask students to explain the answers. Answer any questions about the activity.

2. *Pair work.* Have students take turns asking and answering questions about the pictures.

3. Ask volunteers to read their answers for the class to check.

> **Answers:**
>
> 1. A: What <u>are those</u>?
>   B: <u>They're camcorders</u>.
> 2. A: What <u>are those</u>?
>   B: <u>They're laptops</u>.
> 3. A: What <u>are these</u>?
>   B: <u>They're maps</u>.
> 4. A: What <u>are these</u>?
>   B: <u>They're rulers</u>.
> 5. A: What <u>are these</u>?
>   B: <u>They're pens</u>.
> 6. A: What <u>are those</u>?
>   B: <u>They're chairs</u>.

9 Conversation

Class CD, Track 26

Activity A

1. Focus students' attention on the picture. Ask them to say where they think the men are, what they're doing, and what they're talking about.

2. Have students read the directions for the activity.

3. Play Class CD Track 26 or read the conversation twice.

   Audio script

   A: May I help you?

   B: Yes, please. Where are the CD players?

   A: They're on the wall.

   B: What are those?

   A: They're DVD players. They're really good. And these speakers are really good, too.

   B: Are they expensive?

   A: No, they're on sale.

4. *Pair work.* Have students read the conversation, switching roles.

5. Ask several pairs to demonstrate for the class.

   Also on Student CD, Track 7

Notes

Explain that *on sale* means that an item is being sold for less than its usual price.

Activity B

1. Have students read the directions for the activity. Explain that they will work with a partner and take turns to practice the conversation using their own information. This time they will substitute different objects into the conversation.

2. *Pair work.* Have students do the activity.

3. Ask several pairs to demonstrate for the class.

Student Book pages 18 and 73

10 Communication task:
Where are the headphones?

Activity A

1. Put students in pairs and have them decide who will be Student A and who will be Student B.

Have Student A look at page 18 and Student B look at page 73. Have students read the directions for the activity.

2. Focus students' attention on the picture and the lists of items they will ask about.

3. Focus students' attention on the sample conversation and the picture. Demonstrate the activity with a student volunteer. Make sure everyone understands why Student A will write *1* on the table to represent the location of the laptop.

4. *Pair work.* Have students do the activity. Make sure they understand that they shouldn't show their pictures to their partner.

Activity B

1. Have students read the directions for the activity.

2. *Pair work.* Have students compare their pictures and see if the numbers for the objects are in the correct places.

3. To check answers, make a simple drawing on the board of the picture in the book. Have a student volunteer ask where one of the items is and another student draw it in the correct location on the board. Continue with the rest of the items and different students.

Extra

1. Have students read the directions for the activity.

2. Focus students' attention on the sample sentences.

3. *Pair work.* Have students look at their picture for 30 seconds, close their books, and take turns telling their partner what they remember.

Extension

1. Have students repeat the Extra activity with another page in the book. Alternatively, have them close their eyes and describe the classroom.

2. Put students in pairs and have them sit back-to-back. Have them take turns describing the location of objects in a room and drawing what their partner says. Then have students show their picture to their partner to check their answers.

Check your English

To review the vocabulary and grammar from Unit 3, have students do page 79. This page can be done individually, in pairs, or as a class. It can also be assigned for homework. Alternatively, administer this page as a test at the end of the unit.

Answers:

A   Vocabulary
1. cell phone
2. map
3. headphones
4. eraser
5. DVD player
6. camcorder
7. karaoke machine
8. desk

B   Grammar
1. <u>What's</u> this?
   d. It's an electronic dictionary.
2. <u>Is</u> this your digital camera?
   a. No, it isn't.
3. <u>Where</u> are your books?
   c. They're on the chair.
4. <u>Are</u> these your headphones?
   e. Yes, they are.
5. What are <u>those</u>?
   f. They're speakers.
6. Does he have <u>this</u> video game system?
   b. Yes, he does.

Everyday activities

Unit 4

Components

Student Book: pages 19–24; 74

Check your English: page 80

Class CD: tracks 27–34

Student CD: tracks 8 and 9

Target language

Vocabulary: Daily activities: studying, eating, sleeping; locations and places

Grammar: Present continuous: statements, *Wh-* questions; *at*

Themes: Everyday activities; places

Student Book page 19

Warm-up and review

1. Divide the class into pairs. Have them take turns asking each other what they have on their desks at home: *Do you have a computer on your desk? Yes, I do / No, I don't.*

2. Ask students to tell the class what their partner has on his/her desk.

1 Speaking

Class CD, Track 27

Presentation

1. Focus students' attention on the pictures and text below each one. Explain that they will hear the terms on the CD.

2. Focus students' attention on the pictures again. Have students describe what they see.

Activity A

1. Have students read the directions for the activity.

2. Focus students' attention on the pictures and the text below them. Play Class CD Track 27. Have students listen and look at the pictures. Have students repeat. Go over any words they don't know.

   Audio script

sleeping	studying	reading e-mail
shopping	drinking	driving
cooking dinner	going to work	
talking on the phone	playing the piano	
washing dishes	taking a shower	

3. Explain to students that they will take turns asking and answering questions about what the people in the pictures are doing.

4. Model the sample conversation with a student volunteer.

5. *Pair work.* Have students do the activity.

6. Ask students questions about the pictures to check understanding.

Notes

Make sure students understand that if the question is in the present continuous (*-ing*), then the answer is in the present continuous as well.

Activity B

1. Have students read the directions for the activity.

2. Explain to students that they will act out one of the activities from the pictures at the top of the page. Then they will ask their partner to guess what they are doing.

3. *Pair work.* Focus students' attention on the speech bubbles. Have students do the activity.

4. Have students act out the activities for the class and ask the question. Have the class guess. Have the class vote on who does the best acting for each activity.

2 Listening

Class CD, Track 28

1. Have students read the directions for the activity.

2. Explain to students that they will listen to people talk about activities and write the letter of the correct activity for each person. Read the names and answer choices aloud.

3. Play the first conversation on Class CD Track 28. Make sure everyone understands why the correct answer is *e*. Play the rest of the recording. Have students do the activity. Play the recording again if necessary.

Audio script

1.

A: Hello.

B: Hi, Mike. This is Bob. What are you doing?

A: I'm washing the dishes. What about you?

2.

A: Hello.

B: Hello, Mary. It's Ken. Are you busy?

A: Uh, kind of … I'm cooking dinner.

3.

A: Hello.

B: Hi, Anne. This is Jack.

A: Jack! Where are you?

B: At the mall. I'm shopping for a new TV.

4.

A: Hello.

B: Hey, Kim. It's Ron.

A: Oh, hi, Ron. Where are you?

B: I'm at home. What are you doing?

A: I'm reading. What about you?

5.

A: Hello.

B: Susan, it's Justin.

A: Oh, hi, Justin.

B: What are you doing?

A: I'm studying.

4. Ask volunteers to read their answers for the class to check.

> **Answers:**
>
> 1. **e**   2. **c**   3. **a**   4. **d**   5. **b**

Student Book page 20

3 Grammar: Present continuous

Class CD, Track 29

1. Have students read the directions for the activity.

2. Have students look at the grammar box. Give them time to read the examples.

3. Focus students' attention on the **Memo**. Read the information with students and answer any questions.

4. Play Class CD Track 29. Have students listen. Play the recording again and have students repeat.

Audio script

A: I'm eating. I'm not singing.

B: You're eating. You aren't singing.

A: She's eating. She isn't singing.

B: We're eating. We aren't singing.

A: They're eating. They aren't singing.

A: Are you eating?

B: Yes, I am.

C: No, I'm not.

A: Is she eating?

B: Yes, she is.

C: No, she isn't. / No, she's not.

A: Are they eating?

B: Yes, they are.

C: No, they aren't. / No, they're not.

5. Have a student volunteer pantomime doing one of the activities from page 19. Have them say *I'm (eating). I'm not (singing).* Point to the first student and ask other student volunteers *Is he (eating)?* and have them answer. Continue with other students pantomiming activities and practicing the statements, questions, and answers from the grammar box.

Notes

Remind students that the short answer *Yes, I am* cannot be contracted to *Yes, I'm.* Also, remind students that the intonation of Yes/No questions goes up at the end.

4 Conversation

Class CD, Track 30

Activity A

1. Focus students' attention on the picture. Ask them to say where they think the people are, what they're doing, or what they're saying to each other.

2. Have students read the directions for the activity.

3. Play Class CD Track 30 or read the conversation twice.

Audio script

A: Hello.

B: Hi, Sana. It's me, Nick.

A: Oh, hi, Nick.

B: What are you doing? Are you studying?

A: No, I'm not studying. I'm exercising. What are you doing?

B: Nothing much. Just reading my e-mail.

4. *Pair work*. Have students read the conversation, switching roles.

5. Ask several pairs to demonstrate for the class.

   Also on Student CD, Track 8

Notes

Explain that *Nothing much* is an informal way to express that nothing special or out of the ordinary is happening.

Activity B

1. Have students read the directions for the activity. Explain that they will work with a partner and take turns to practice the conversation using their own information. This time they will talk about different activities and substitute them in the conversation.

2. *Pair work*. Have students do the activity.

3. Ask several pairs to demonstrate for the class. To make the conversation more realistic, have students stand facing away from each other as they say the conversation.

Extra

Have students change partners and repeat Activity B.

Extension

1. Give students time to think of other activities and how to pantomime them. Allow them to use their dictionaries if necessary. Then have them repeat Activity B.

2. Have students play Charades. Divide the class into small groups. Have one student pantomime one of the actions and the other students guess the activity.

Student Book pages 21 and 74

5 Communication task:
What's the difference?

Activity A

1. Put students in pairs and have them decide who will be Student A and who will be Student B. Have Student A look at page 21 and Student B look at page 74. Have students read the directions for the activity.

2. Focus attention on the picture. To check understanding, ask students, *Where are the people?* Then ask Student A and Student B, *Who is playing the piano?*

3. Have students do the activity individually. Make sure they take notes about each person in the picture. Tell them not to look at each other's picture or notes.

Activity B

1. Have students read the directions for the activity.

2. *Pair work*. Have student take turns asking each other about the activities of each person in the picture. Tell them to take notes about the differences.

3. Have several pairs tell the class about one difference between the pictures until all the differences have been mentioned. Have students check their answers.

Extra

1. Have students read the directions for the activity.

2. Have both students look at the picture on page 74. Tell the A students to memorize as much as they can in 30 seconds.

3. *Pair work*. Have the A students close their books and tell their partner as much as they can remember about the people in Student B's picture.

4. Have students reverse roles: Student B looks at Student A's picture for 30 seconds and tells Student A as much as she/he can remember.

Places

Warm-up and review

Write different activities on separate slips of paper and put them in a bag. Have several students choose a paper and pantomime the activity. Quickly go around the class and ask what the students are doing.

6 Speaking

Class CD, Track 31

Presentation

1. Focus students' attention on the pictures and the text below each one. Explain that they will hear the terms on the CD.

2. Focus students' attention on the pictures again. Have students describe what they see.

Activity A

1. Have students read the directions for the activity.

2. Focus students' attention on the pictures and the text below them. Play Class CD Track 31. Have students listen and look at the pictures. Have students repeat. Go over any words they don't know.

    Audio script

in a store	at home	at work
at a theater	at school	on a street

3. Explain to students that they will take turns asking and answering questions about where the people are in the pictures.

4. Make sure students pay special attention to the prepositional phrases for each place. Make sure they understand that these words are usually not interchangeable.

5. Model the sample conversation with a student volunteer.

6. *Pair work.* Have students do the activity.

7. Ask students questions about the pictures to check understanding.

Activity B

1. Have students read the directions for the activity.

2. Explain to students that they will now talk with their partner about what the people in the pictures are doing.

3. *Pair work.* Focus students' attention on the speech bubble. Have them do the activity.

4. Have students tell the class what is happening in each picture for the class to check answers.

7 Listening

Class CD, Track 32

Activity A

1. Have students read the directions for the activity.

2. Explain to students that they will listen to people talk about where people are. Students will then circle the correct answer for the question, *Where are the people in the photos?*

3. Read the answer choices aloud and check that students understand each one.

4. Play the first conversation on Class CD Track 32. Make sure everyone understands why the correct answer is *a*. Play the rest of the recording. Have students do the activity. Play the recording again if necessary.

    Audio script

    I.
    A: Jenny, who are the people in this picture?
    B: They're my parents.
    A: Where are they?
    B: They're in a restaurant.
    A: What are they doing? Are they singing?
    B: Yes, they are!

    2.
    A: Is that you, Mark?
    B: Yes, it is.
    A: Where are you?
    B: I'm at a party.
    A: What are you doing?
    B: I'm sleeping.

3.

A: Who are those people, Lucy?

B: They're my cousins.

A: Where are they?

B: They're at a birthday party.

A: Oh, yeah. They're eating birthday cake.

4.

A: Those children are cute. Where are they?

B: They're at school.

A: What are they doing?

B: They're exercising.

5.

A: Charlie, is that your sister?

B: Yes, it is.

A: Is she in a restaurant?

B: No, she's at home.

A: What's she doing in the picture?

B: She's cooking.

6.

A: Meg, who's that man?

B: That's my uncle Joe.

A: Where is he?

B: At work.

A: What's he doing? Is he talking on the phone?

B: Yes, he is.

5. Ask volunteers to read their answers for the class to check.

> **Answers:**
>
> 1. **a.** in a restaurant
> 2. **a.** at a party
> 3. **a.** at a party
> 4. **a.** at school
> 5. **b.** at home
> 6. **b.** at work

Activity B

1. Have students read the directions for the activity.

2. Explain to students that they will listen to the CD again and check if the statements are true or false.

3. Read the answer choices aloud and check that students understand each one.

4. Play the first conversation on the recording again. Make sure everyone understands why the correct answer is *true*. Play the rest of the recording again and have students do the activity.

5. Ask volunteers to read their answers for the class to check.

> **Answers:**
>
> 1. True
> 2. False
> 3. False
> 4. True
> 5. False
> 6. True

Student Book page 23

8 Grammar: *Wh-* questions in the present continuous; preposition *at*

Class CD, Track 33

Activity A

1. Have students read the directions for the activity.

2. Have students look at the pictures. Ask volunteers what each person is doing.

3. Give students time to read the questions and answers under each picture. Focus attention on the question words *what*, *where*, and *who*. To check understanding, ask students various questions about their classmates such as *Who's sitting next to the window? Where's (Yumi) sitting? What's (Ken) wearing?*

4. Play Class CD Track 33. Have students listen. Play the recording again and have students repeat.

    Audio script

    A: What's Eric doing?

    B: Sleeping.

    A: Where's he sleeping?

    B: At home.

    A: What's Beth doing?

    B: Reading.

    A: What's she reading?

    B: Her e-mail.

    A: Who's eating?

    B: Paulo is.

    A: What's he eating?

    B: Dinner.

5. Ask various students the questions under each of the pictures to check understanding.

Activity B

1. Focus students' attention on the pictures. Ask students what the person in each picture is doing.

2. Have students read the directions for the activity. Focus attention on the speech bubbles. Model the questions and answers and have students repeat.

3. *Pair work.* Have students take turns asking and answering questions about the pictures using *who*, *what*, and *where* and the present continuous.

4. Have several pairs demonstrate their conversations for the class.

9 Conversation

Class CD, Track 34

Activity A

1. Focus students' attention on the picture. Ask them to say where they think the people are and what they are doing.

2. Have students read the directions for the activity.

3. Play Class CD Track 34 or read the conversation twice.

Audio script

A: Hello.
B: Hi, Bart. It's Kate. What are you doing?
A: Studying. Where are you?
B: At home. So, tell me … what are you studying?
A: English. I have a big test.
B: Where's Ben? Is he at home?
A: Yeah, he is, but he's sleeping.

4. *Pair work.* Have students read the conversation, switching roles.

5. Ask several pairs to demonstrate for the class.

Also on Student CD, Track 9

Notes

Explain that *So, tell me…* is an informal conversational way to change the subject. *Big test* is an informal way to say that the test is important and/or difficult.

Activity B

1. Have students read the directions for the activity. Explain that they will work with a partner and take turns saying each part in the conversation from Activity A. This time they will imagine that they're doing different activities and substitute them in the conversation.

2. *Pair work.* Have students do the activity.

3. Ask several pairs to demonstrate for the class. To make the conversation more realistic, have students stand facing away from each other as they say the conversation.

Student Book page 24

10 Communication task:
At the station

Activity A

1. Have students read the directions for the activity. Have students point to each person and say what they are doing.

2. Focus students' attention on the sample conversation and the picture. Model the sample conversation with a student volunteer.

3. *Pair work.* Have students take turns asking questions and guessing who the other person is talking about. Make sure students understand that the questions should all be Yes/No.

4. Have several pairs demonstrate one of their conversations for the class.

Activity B

1. Have students read the directions for the activity. Focus students' attention on the sample conversation and the picture. Model the sample conversation with a student volunteer.

2. To check understanding, have several volunteers ask a *Wh-* question about the picture.

3. *Pair work.* Have students take turns asking *Wh-* questions about the picture.

4. Have several pairs demonstrate one of their conversations for the class.

Extra

1. Have students read the directions for the activity.

2. Have students look at the picture for 30 seconds. Tell them to memorize as much as they can.

3. *Pair work.* Have students take turns saying one sentence about what the people are doing in the picture.

4. Ask volunteers to say one sentence about the picture for the class to check.

Extension

Have several students stand up and pantomime different activities for about 20 seconds. Have the other students try to remember what the students are doing, without taking notes. Have students ask each other about what the other students did.

Check your English

To review the vocabulary and grammar from Unit 4, have students do page 80. This page can be done individually, in pairs, or as a class. It can also be assigned for homework. Alternatively, administer this page as a test at the end of the unit.

Answers:

A Vocabulary
1. exercise
2. play the piano
3. cook
4. read
5. talk on the phone
6. sleep
7. ride (a motor scooter)
8. shop

B Grammar
1. **e.** She's reading her English book.
2. **c.** No, I'm not. I'm watching a DVD.
3. **b.** He's studying Chinese.
4. **d.** No, they aren't. They're studying.
5. **g.** I'm at school.
6. **h.** No, he's not. He's exercising.
7. **a.** No, she's not. She's at home.
8. **f.** Yes, we're studying English.

Foods and drinks

Components

Student Book: pages 25–30

Check your English: page 81

Class CD: tracks 35–42

Student CD: tracks 12 and 13

Target language

Vocabulary: Food, beverages, meals, restaurant vocabulary; snack foods; *a lot*

Grammar: Simple present; agreeing and disagreeing; count and noncount nouns; *How much / How many*

Themes: Foods and drinks; snacks

Student Book page 25

Warm-up and review

Play Charades. Have students take turns acting out one of the activities from Unit 4 and have the other students guess. Do the activity as a class or in small groups.

1 Speaking

Class CD, Track 35

Presentation

Focus students' attention on the pictures and the text below each one. Explain that they will hear the terms on the CD.

Activity A

1. Have students read the directions for the activity.

2. Focus students' attention on the pictures and the text below them. Play Class CD Track 35. Have students listen and look at the pictures. Have students repeat. Go over any words they don't know.

   ### Audio script

apples	chicken	cake	carrots
coffee	french fries	ice cream	pie
salad	soda	soup	spaghetti
steak	tea	tomatoes	

3. Explain to students that they will take turns asking and answering questions about the pictures.

4. Model the sample conversation with a student volunteer.

5. *Pair work.* Have students do the activity.

6. Ask students questions about the pictures to check understanding.

Notes

Make sure students understand that *Do you (eat apples)?* is asking if the person does something on a regular basis, not just once or twice.

Activity B

1. Have students read the directions for the activity.

2. Explain to students that they will use the pictures at the top of the page as cues to take turns asking each other what foods and drinks they like.

3. *Pair work.* Focus students' attention on the speech bubble. Have them do the activity.

4. Have students tell the class which foods and drinks their partner likes and doesn't like.

5. Conduct a class poll to see which are the favorite foods and least favorite foods.

2 Listening

Class CD, Track 36

1. Have students read the directions for the activity.

2. Explain to students that they will listen to a woman ordering a meal in a restaurant and check what she orders.

3. Focus attention on the column heads. Make sure students understand what these categories mean.

4. Play the first section of Class CD Track 36 (through *Yes, please. The house salad.*). Make sure everyone understands why the correct answer for **Appetizer** is *house salad*. Play the rest of the recording. Have students do the activity. Play the recording again if necessary.

Audio script

A: Are you ready to order?

B: Yes.

A: Can I get you an appetizer?

B: Yes, please. The house salad.

A: OK. And for your main course?

B: Spaghetti with tomato sauce, please.

A: Anything to drink?

B: Coffee, please.

A: Any dessert?

B: Oh, yes. Ice cream for dessert!

5. Ask volunteers to read their answers for the class to check.

> **Answers:**
>
> Appetizers: house salad
> Main course: spaghetti with tomato sauce
> Beverages: coffee
> Desserts: ice cream

Notes

Explain that a *house salad* means a regular salad with no special ingredients. It's usually made with lettuce, tomato, and maybe a couple more vegetables. At many restaurants in the U.S., a house salad is included in the price of the main course.

Student Book page 26

3 Grammar: Simple present; agreeing and disagreeing

Class CD, Track 37

1. Have students read the directions for the activity.

2. Have students look at the grammar box. Give them time to read the examples.

3. Play Class CD Track 37. Have students listen. Play the recording again and have students repeat.

Audio script

A: I like chicken. I don't like steak.

B: You like chicken. You don't like steak.

A: He likes chicken. He doesn't like steak.

B: She likes chicken. She doesn't like steak.

A: We like chicken. We don't like steak.

B: They like chicken. They don't like steak.

A: Do you like chicken?

B: Yes, I do.

C: No, I don't.

A: Does he like chicken?

B: Yes, he does.

C: No, he doesn't.

A: Do they like chicken?

B: Yes, they do.

C: No, they don't.

Agreeing

A: I do, too.

B: He does, too.

A: They do, too.

A: I don't either.

B: He doesn't either.

A: They don't either.

Disagreeing

A: I don't.

B: He doesn't.

A: They don't.

4. In order to review agreeing and disagreeing, ask a volunteer to say one of the foods on page 25. Ask the volunteer if he/she like it. Ask another student about the first student, then add your own agreement or disagreement. For example:

> S1: *Apples.*
> S: *Do you like apples?*
> T: *No, I don't.*
>
> T: *Does (Bo-wei) like apples?*
> S: *No, he doesn't.*
> T: *I don't either.*

Ask various students the questions in the grammar box and encourage them to practice agreeing and disagreeing as above.

Notes

Remind students that the intonation of Yes/No questions goes up at the end.

4 Conversation

Class CD, Track 38

Activity A

1. Focus students' attention on the photo. Ask them to say where they think the people are, what they're doing, or what they're saying to each other.

2. Have students read the directions for the activity.

3. Focus students' attention on the **Memo**. Read the information with students and answer any questions.

4. Play Class CD Track 38 or read the conversation twice.

Audio script

A: Do you like Italian food?

B: Oh, yes. I love it!

A: I do, too. I know a nice Italian restaurant. It's called Luigi's.

B: Do they have pizza?

A: Oh, yeah. The pizza is great. And the spaghetti's good, too.

B: Where is it?

A: It's on Prince Street.

B: OK. Let's go!

5. *Pair work.* Have students read the conversation, switching roles.

6. Ask several pairs to demonstrate for the class.

Also on Student CD, Track 10

Notes

Explain to students that *I know a nice (Italian) restaurant* is a common way to make a suggestion about where to eat. The phrase can also be used to make other kinds of suggestions such as *I know a nice park/cafe/store.*

Activity B

1. Have students read the directions for the activity. Explain that they will work with a partner and take turns saying each part in the conversation from Activity A. This time they will talk about restaurants they know and substitute true information about themselves.

2. *Pair work.* Have students do the activity.

3. Ask several pairs to demonstrate for the class.

Extra

1. Have students read the directions for the activity.

2. Explain to students that they will take turns asking and answering questions about their likes and dislikes until they find two things they both like and two things they don't like to eat and drink.

3. *Pair work.* Have students do the activity.

4. Have students share their partner's answers with the class.

Extension

1. Give students time to think of other foods and drinks. Allow them to use their dictionaries if necessary.

2. Put students in pairs and have them take turns asking each other if they like the new food items.

Student Book page 27

5 Communication task:
At a restaurant

Activity A

1. Have students read the directions for the activity.

2. Focus students' attention on the menu. Explain any vocabulary that students don't understand. To check understanding, ask students questions such as *What's in a Greek salad? Does a fish filet have bones? Have you ever eaten chocolate mousse? Did you like it?*

3. Have students do the activity.

Notes

You may need to explain some of the dishes listed on the menu. Here are some brief descriptions that may help.

Green salad: this is another name for a house salad (see the Notes section following **2 Listening** on page 30).

Greek salad: this is normally made of tomato, cucumber, onion, green pepper, olives, and feta cheese. In North America, lettuce is also used.

Chocolate mousse: *mousse* is a creamy dessert made from egg, sugar, and cream.

Activity B

1. Have students read the directions for the activity. Ask students what a server at a restaurant does.

2. Focus students' attention on the **Helpful Language** note. Practice the questions by brainstorming appropriate answers with the class.

3. *Pair work.* Have student take turns pretending to be the server and the customer in a restaurant.

4. Have several pairs demonstrate their role-play for the class.

Notes

You may want to explain that the term *server* means waiter or waitress. It is gender neutral, and is becoming more widely used in the U.S. than waiter and waitress.

Extension

Put students in groups of three or four. Have them work together to write a new menu. Then have them take turns pretending to be the server and customers.

Snacks

Warm-up and review

On the board write the foods and drinks from page 25 with scrambled letters (*feofce = coffee*). Put students in pairs and have them unscramble the words. Then have them take turns asking each other if they like or don't like each item.

6 Speaking

Class CD, Track 39

Presentation

1. Focus students' attention on the pictures and the text below each one. Explain that they will hear the terms on the CD.

2. Explain that these foods are snacks, meaning that they are eaten between meals, not as a meal. Elicit other favorite snacks from students and write them on the board (these will be used in Activity B).

Activity A

1. Have students read the directions for the activity.

2. Focus students' attention on the pictures and the text below them. Play Class CD Track 39. Have students listen and look at the pictures. Have students repeat. Go over any words they don't know.

   #### Audio script

chocolate	cookies	fruit	nuts
popcorn	potato chips	pretzels	rice cakes

3. Explain to students that they will take turns asking and answering questions about the snacks in the pictures.

4. Model the sample conversation with a student volunteer.

5. *Pair work.* Have students do the activity.

6. Ask students questions about the pictures to check understanding.

Activity B

1. Have students read the directions for the activity.

2. Explain to students that they will now talk with their partner about their favorite snacks.

3. *Pair work.* Focus students' attention on the speech bubble. Have students do the activity. Remind them of the snacks that were brainstormed in the "Presentation" section in case their favorite snacks are not pictured.

4. Have students tell the class about their partner's favorite snacks. Discuss who likes the most unusual snacks.

7 Listening

Class CD, Track 40

Activity A

1. Focus students' attention on the picture. Ask them to say where they think the people are and what they're doing. Elicit the names of the food shown in the picture (*cheese, popcorn, potato chips*, etc.).

2. Have students read the directions for the activity.

3. Explain to students that they will listen to people talk about snacks and then circle the correct answer to the question, *What foods or beverages are they talking about?* Read the answer choices aloud and answer any questions about vocabulary.

4. Play the first question on Class CD Track 40. Make sure everyone understands why the correct answer is *b*. Have students do the activity. Play the recording again if necessary.

   #### Audio script

   1. What kind of ice cream does Miya like?
   2. Do you want some cake?
   3. I love chocolate. Do you like chocolate?
   4. Does Jin want some fruit?
   5. Do you and Taro eat nuts?

5. Ask volunteers to read their answers for the class to check.

   Answers:
   1. **b.** ice cream
   2. **c.** cake
   3. **b.** chocolate
   4. **a.** fruit
   5. **c.** nuts

Activity B

1. Have students read the directions for the activity.

2. Explain to students that they will listen to the CD again and circle what they think each person will say next. Read the answer choices aloud and answer any questions about vocabulary.

3. Play the first question on the recording again. Make sure everyone understands why the correct answer is *b*. Play the rest of the recording again. Have students do the activity.

4. Ask volunteers to read their answers for the class to check.

> **Answers:**
> 1. **b.** She likes chocolate.
> 2. **b.** No, thank you.
> 3. **b.** Yes, I do.
> 4. **a.** Yes, he does.
> 5. **a.** No, we don't.

Student Book page 29

8 Grammar:
Count and noncount nouns

Class CD, Track 41

Activity A

1. Have students read the directions for the activity.

2. Have students look at the grammar box. Give them time to read the examples.

3. Play Class CD Track 41. Have students listen. Play the recording again and have students repeat.

Audio script

A: Do you eat much popcorn?

B: No, not much.

A: I don't drink much coffee.

B: I drink a lot of tea.

A: How many pretzels do you eat?

B: Not many.

A: I don't eat many snacks.

B: I eat a lot of fruit.

4. Have a student volunteer point to one of the food pictures on page 28 or draw it quickly on the board. Have students use the grammar in the box to talk about it. For example, *Do you eat much chocolate? Yes, I do. How much chocolate do you eat?*

Notes

1. Explain to students that a count noun is usually an object with a consistent size and shape that is easy to count, such as an apple, a cookie, etc. Noncount nouns can usually change their shape or size depending on what container they are in (coffee), or the individual pieces are so small that it is not practical to count them (popcorn).

2. Explain to students that *how many* is used with count nouns and *how much* is used with noncount nouns.

Activity B

1. Have students read the directions for the activity.

2. Focus students' attention on the list of foods and drinks. Ask students to say if each one is a count or noncount noun.

3. Focus students' attention on the speech bubbles. Model the questions and answers and have students repeat.

4. *Pair work.* Have students do the activity.

5. Have several pairs demonstrate their conversations for the class.

9 Conversation

Class CD, Track 42

Activity A

1. Focus students' attention on the picture. Ask them to guess where the women are, what they're doing, or what they're saying to each other.

2. Have students read the directions for the activity.

3. Play Class CD Track 42 or read the conversation twice.

Audio script

A: Do you like chocolate?

B: I love chocolate! Do you like chocolate?

A: Yeah, I do. How much chocolate do you eat?

B: I eat a lot! I eat some every day.

A: Do you eat many chocolate bars?

B: No, I don't eat many chocolate bars, but I eat a lot of chocolate cookies and ice cream.

4. *Pair work.* Have students read the conversation, switching roles.

5. Ask several pairs to demonstrate for the class.

   Also on Student CD, Track 11

Notes

Explain that *a lot* can be used with count or noncount nouns.

Activity B

1. Have students read the directions for the activity. Explain that they will work with a partner and take turns saying each part in the conversation from Activity A. This time they will substitute true information about themselves.

2. *Pair work.* Have students do the activity.

3. Ask several pairs to demonstrate for the class.

Extra

1. Put students in pairs and have them read the directions for the activity and the examples.

2. Have partners do the activity.

Student Book page 30

10 Communication task:
What are they eating?

Activity A

1. Have students read the directions for the activity. Have students point to each person and say what they are eating.

2. Focus students' attention on the sample conversation and the first picture. Model the sample conversation with a student volunteer.

3. *Pair work.* Have students do the activity.

4. Have several pairs demonstrate one of their conversations to the class.

Activity B

1. Have students read the directions for the activity. Focus attention on the sample sentences.

2. To check understanding, have several volunteers say a sentence about one of the pictures.

3. *Pair work.* Give students about 30 seconds to look at the pictures. Then have them cover the page. Have them take turns saying one sentence about the people in the pictures.

4. Have students say a sentence for the rest of the class to check their answers.

Extra

1. Have students read the example and the directions for the activity.

2. Put students in groups of three or four. Have students discuss what foods their friends and family like and don't like.

Extension

Have a class discussion about favorite foods and recipes. Ask students if they like to cook and what kinds of things they make. Ask students if there are any foods they have never tried but would like to try, and if there is any food that they would never try.

Student Book page 81

Check your English

To review the vocabulary and grammar from Unit 5, have students do page 81. This page can be done individually, in pairs, or as a class. It can also be assigned for homework. Alternatively, administer this page as a test at the end of the unit.

Answers:

A Vocabulary

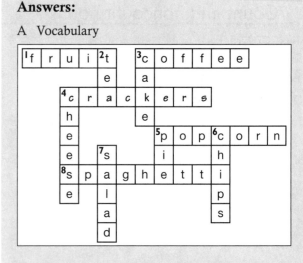

B Grammar
1. A: much
   B: A lot
2. cooks
3. doesn't
4. eat
5. don't

Components

Student Book: pages 31–36; 75

Check your English: page 82

Class CD: tracks 43–50

Student CD: tracks 12 and 13

Target language

Vocabulary: House, apartment, rooms; furniture

Grammar: *There is / there are*; prepositions of place

Themes: Housing; furniture

Student Book page 31

Warm-up and review

1. Remind students of the Unit 5 themes: foods, drinks, and snacks.

2. *Pair work.* Divide the class into pairs. Give students three or four minutes to talk about their favorite foods, drinks, and snacks.

3. Have volunteers tell the class about their favorites. This can be conducted as a poll to see what the class favorites are.

1 Speaking

Class CD, Track 43

Presentation

1. Focus students' attention on the picture and the list of vocabulary next to it. Explain that they will hear the terms on the CD.

2. Focus students' attention on the picture. Ask students if the house is similar to or different from their house/apartment.

3. Focus students' attention on the labels *First Floor* and *Second Floor.* Make sure students understand what they mean.

Activity A

1. Have students read the directions for the activity.

2. Focus students' attention on the picture and the list of vocabulary next to it. Play Class CD Track 43. Have students listen and look at the picture. Have students repeat. Go over any words they don't know.

Audio script

1.	living room	7.	yard
2.	stairs	8.	balcony
3.	dining room	9.	bedroom
4.	terrace	10.	hall
5.	kitchen	11.	closet
6.	garage	12.	bathroom

3. Explain to students that they will take turns asking and answering questions about the house in the picture.

4. Model the sample conversation with a student volunteer.

5. *Pair work.* Have students do the activity.

6. Ask students questions about the picture to check understanding.

Activity B

1. Have students read the directions for the activity.

2. Explain to students that they will take turns asking each other what their favorite room is.

3. *Pair work.* Focus students' attention on the speech bubble. Have them do the activity.

4. Have students tell the class what their partner's favorite room is.

2 Listening

Class CD, Track 44

1. Have students read the directions for the activity.

2. Explain to students that they will listen to people talk about apartments and number the correct picture.

3. Focus attention on the pictures. Have students point to the rooms in each picture and say what they are.

4. Play the first conversation on Class CD Track 44. Make sure everyone understands why picture *a* is labeled *b*. Play the rest of the recording. Have students do the activity. Play the recording again if necessary.

Audio script

1.

A: Do you like your new apartment, Zai?

B: Oh, I love it! It's really big.

A: How many bedrooms does it have?

B: Two. And it has a living room, a big kitchen, and a bathroom.

2.

A: How's your new apartment, Joan?

B: Well, it's cute, but it's really small. It has only one room and a bathroom.

A: Really? You don't have a bedroom?

B: No, I sleep in the living room.

3.

A: Do you like your new apartment, Neil?

B: Not really. It's too small.

A: Really? It's too small?

B: Yeah. One bedroom, a small kitchen, and a living room.

5. Ask volunteers to read their answers for the class to check.

Answers:

a. 2   b. 1   c. 3

Notes

Explain that a one-room apartment is called a *studio apartment* in the U.S.

Extension

Play Track 44 again. Have students say if each speaker likes their apartment, and why or why not.

Student Book page 32

3 Grammar: *There is / there are*

Class CD, Track 45

1. Have students read the directions for the activity.

2. Have students look at the grammar box. Give them time to read the examples.

3. Make sure students understand that *there is* is used for singular objects and *there are* is used for plural objects.

4. Focus students' attention on the **Memo**. Read the information with students and answer any questions.

5. Play Class CD Track 45. Have students listen. Play the recording again and have students repeat.

Audio script

A: There's a bathroom on the second floor.

B: There are some closets in the bedroom.

A: There's no bathroom on the first floor.

B: There are no closets in the hall.

A: There isn't a bathroom on the first floor.

B: There aren't any closets in the hall.

A: Is there a yard?

B: Yes, there is.

C: No, there isn't.

A: Are there any stairs?

B: Yes, there are.

C: No, there aren't.

6. Have students look at the picture of the house on page 31. Have volunteers say one sentence about the house using *there is* or *there are*.

Notes

1. Remind students that the answer *Yes, there is* cannot be contracted to *Yes, there's*.

2. Explain that *some* is only used in affirmative statements (*There are some windows in the kitchen.*), and *any* is used in negative statements (*There aren't any windows in the kitchen.*) or questions (*Are there any windows in the kitchen?*).

4 Conversation

Class CD, Track 46

Activity A

1. Focus students' attention on the photo. Ask them to say where they think the people are, what they're doing, or what the people are saying to each other.

2. Have students read the directions for the activity.

3. Play Class CD Track 46 or read the conversation twice.

Audio script

A: Oh, I like your new apartment, Daisy. It's really nice!

B: Thanks. I like it because it's big.

A: How many bedrooms are there?

B: There are two. And there's a living room, a kitchen, and a big bathroom.

A: Nice! And how many closets are there?

B: A lot. There are four big closets.

A: Wow! Is there a balcony?

B: No, there isn't, but there's a small yard.

A: That's great!

4. *Pair work.* Have students read the conversation, switching roles.

5. Ask several pairs to demonstrate for the class.

   Also on Student CD, Track 12

Notes

Explain that *That's great* is an informal way to say that something is very good.

Activity B

1. Have students read the directions for the activity. Explain that they will work with a partner and take turns to practice the conversation using their own information. This time they will substitute true information about their own house or apartment in the conversation.

2. Focus students' attention on the **Helpful Language** note. Practice the questions by brainstorming appropriate answers with the class.

3. *Pair work.* Have partners do the activity.

4. Ask several pairs to demonstrate for the class.

Extra

1. Have students read the examples and the directions for the activity.

2. Have students tell the class about their partner's house or apartment.

Student Book page 33

5 Communication task:
My dream house

Activity A

1. Have students read the directions for the activity. Ask them what *dream house* means.

2. Focus students' attention on the picture and the questions. Preteach the phrase *special features*.

3. Elicit vocabulary from students about the house in the picture. Ask them to name what they see. For example, *a pool, a patio, a yard.*

4. To check understanding, ask the questions to several students. Brainstorm any additional vocabulary students need to describe their dream home.

5. Have students do the activity.

Activity B

1. Have students read the directions for the activity.

2. Focus students' attention on the pictures and captions. Have students describe the pictures.

3. Focus students' attention on the **Helpful Language** note. Brainstorm other ways to describe a dream home. Encourage students to also use the questions in the **Helpful Language** note on page 32.

4. *Pair work.* Have students take turns asking each other about their dream home.

5. Have several pairs demonstrate their conversation for the class.

Extra

1. Have students read the examples and the directions for the activity.

2. Have students tell the class about their partner's dream house.

In an apartment

Warm-up and review

Put students in pairs and have them take turns describing their houses or apartments to each other.

6 Speaking

Class CD, Track 47

Presentation

1. Focus students' attention on the pictures and the text below each one. Explain that they will hear the terms on the CD.

2. Focus students' attention on the pictures again. Ask them if they have any of these items in their home.

Activity A

1. Have students read the directions for the activity.

2. Focus students' attention on the pictures and the text below them. Play Class CD Track 47. Have students listen and look at the pictures. Have students repeat. Go over any words they don't know.

   Audio script

   | armchair | bed | picture | coffee table |
   | dresser | lamp | bookcase | sofa |

3. Explain to students that they will take turns asking and answering questions about the pictures.

4. Model the sample conversation with a student volunteer.

5. *Pair work.* Have students do the activity.

6. Ask students questions about the pictures to check understanding.

Activity B

1. Explain to students that they will now talk with their partner about the furniture in their bedroom.

2. *Pair work.* Focus students' attention on the speech bubble. Have students do the activity.

3. Have students tell the class about their partner's bedroom furniture.

7 Listening

Class CD, Track 48

Activity A

1. Have students read the directions for the activity.

2. Explain to students that they will listen to people talk about their bedrooms and number the objects in the correct order. Explain that they will listen to the speakers and choose the correct answer for the question, *What objects don't they have?* Make sure students understand that there is one item that will not be numbered.

3. Play the first speaker on Class CD Track 48. Make sure everyone understands why the correct answer is *bookcase.* Play the rest of the recording. Have students do the activity. Play the recording again if necessary.

   Audio script

   1. My bedroom is very small. I don't have much furniture in it. There's just a bed, a dresser, and a lamp. There's a picture on the dresser. It's a picture of my family.
   2. What's in my bedroom? Well, there's a bed, a dresser, and a bookcase. There's a lamp next to the bookcase, on the floor.
   3. My bedroom is big, but there isn't much furniture. There's a bookcase and a dresser. There isn't a bed. I sleep on the floor.
   4. I have a small bedroom. And it doesn't have much furniture. There's a bed and a lamp. There's a bookcase, too—with a lot of books and pictures, too.

4. Ask volunteers to read their answers for the class to check.

   Answers:
   3 bed
   1 bookcase
   4 dresser
   2 picture

Activity B

1. Have students read the directions for the activity.

2. Explain to students that they will listen to the CD again and check if each statement is true or false.

Read the answer choices aloud and answer any questions about vocabulary.

3. Play the first speaker on Class CD Track 48 again. Make sure everyone understands why the correct answer is *False*. Play the rest of the recording again and have students do the activity.

4. Have volunteers give their answers for the class to check their answers.

> **Answers:**
> 1. False
> 2. True
> 3. False
> 4. True

Extension

Play Track 48 again and ask students to correct the false sentences in Activity B.

> **Answers:**
> 1. There is a picture on the dresser.
> 3. She has no bed.

Student Book page 35

8 Grammar: Prepositions of place

Class CD, Track 49

Activity A

1. Have students read the directions for the activity.

2. Have students look at the sentences under each picture. Give them time to read the examples.

3. Play Class CD Track 49. Have students listen. Play the recording again and have students repeat.

> **Audio script**
>
> A: The clock is on top of the TV.
> B: The pens are on the table.
> A: The lamp is between the armchairs.
> B: The wall is behind the sofa.
> A: The wastebasket is under the table.
> B: The lamp is next to the window.

4. Tell students to take out a pen, a pencil, and an eraser, and put them on their desk. Say a sentence using a preposition and the objects and have students arrange the objects to match the sentence. Then have students take turns saying a sentence for the class.

Activity B

1. Have students read the directions for the activity. Focus their attention on the speech bubble. Model the sentence.

2. *Pair work.* Have students take turns making sentences about objects in the classroom.

3. Have several pairs say their sentences for the class.

9 Conversation

Class CD, Track 50

Activity A

1. Focus students' attention on the picture. Ask them to say where the men are, what they're doing, or what they're saying to each other.

2. Have students read the directions for the activity.

3. Play Class CD Track 50 or read the conversation twice.

> **Audio script**
>
> A: What are you doing?
> B: I'm looking for my cell phone.
> A: It's on the bookcase, on top of the notebook.
> B: Oh, right. And where are my books?
> A: They're on the table.
> B: The table under the window?
> A: No, the table next to the sofa.
> B: Oh, OK. I see them. Thanks!

4. *Pair work.* Have students read the conversation, switching roles.

5. Ask several pairs to demonstrate for the class.

> **Also on Student CD, Track 13**

Activity B

1. Have students read the directions for the activity. Explain that they will work with a partner and take turns to practice the conversation from Activity A. This time they will substitute the objects listed.

2. Focus students' attention on the picture. Ask several students to identify the location of each object in the picture using prepositions.

3. *Pair work.* Have students do the activity.

4. Ask several groups to demonstrate for the class.

10 Communication task:
What's missing?

Activity A

1. Put students in pairs and have them decide who will be Student A and who will be Student B. Have Student A look at page 36 and Student B look at page 75. Have students read the directions for the activity. Ask students what the word *missing* means.

2. Focus attention on the picture. To check understanding, ask students, *How many rooms are there? Are there any pictures in the dining room? Is there a dresser in the bedroom?*

3. Focus students' attention on the labels *Upstairs*, *Downstairs*, and *Outside* on the picture. Make sure students understand what these words mean.

4. Have students do the activity. Make sure they take notes about each room in the house. Tell them not to look at each other's picture or notes.

Activity B

1. Have students read the directions for the activity. Make sure students understand that they will be trying to find five differences between their two pictures, but they cannot look at each other's pictures.

2. Focus students' attention on the **Helpful Language** note. Brainstorm questions that use the language in the note.

3. *Pair work*. Have student take turns asking each other about their pictures. Tell them to take notes about the differences.

4. Have students say one sentence each for the rest of the class to check their answers.

Extension

Have students ask each other about their own houses or apartments and write sentences about the similarities and differences.

Check your English

To review the vocabulary and grammar from Unit 6, have students do page 82. This page can be done individually, in pairs, or as a class. It can also be assigned for homework. Alternatively, administer this page as a test at the end of the unit.

Answers:

A Vocabulary
1. kitchen
2. stairs
3. bed
4. bathroom
5. sofa
6. yard
7. lamp
8. balcony

B Grammar
1. The books are under the chair.
2. There aren't any plants in the room.
3. The headphones are on top of the TV.
4. There is no lamp behind the armchair. / There is no armchair behind the lamp.

Free-time activities

Components

Student Book: pages 37–42

Check your English: page 83

Class CD: tracks 51–58

Student CD: tracks 14 and 15

Target language

Vocabulary: Leisure activities; sports, exercise, hobbies

Grammar: Information questions; adverbs of frequency; *can* for ability

Themes: Free-time activities; popular sports

Student Book page 37

Warm-up and review

Draw a simple picture on the board of a room with various items and furniture in it. Have students describe the location of one of the items (*The lamp is next to the desk. The cat is under the sofa.*). Continue with other students.

1 Speaking

Class CD, Track 51

Presentation

1. Focus students' attention on the pictures and the text below each one. Explain that they will hear the terms on the CD.

2. Focus students' attention on the pictures. Have students describe what they see.

Activity A

1. Have students read the directions for the activity.

2. Focus students' attention on the pictures and the text below them. Play Class CD Track 51. Have students listen and look at the pictures. Have students repeat. Go over any words they don't know.

   Audio script

go to the movies	watch TV
work out at a gym	surf the Internet
take photos	play cards
go dancing	go to the beach
go shopping	listen to music
eat out	paint

3. Explain to students that they will take turns asking and answering questions about the activities in the pictures.

4. Model the conversation with a student volunteer.

5. *Pair work.* Have students do the activity.

6. Ask students questions about the pictures to check understanding.

Notes

Make sure students understand that *free time* is the time that is not spent at work or taking care of responsibilities such as family or housework.

Activity B

1. Have students read the directions for the activity.

2. Explain to students that they will use the pictures at the top of the page as cues to take turns asking each other which activities they like to do and which ones they don't like to do.

3. *Pair work.* Focus students' attention on the speech bubble. Have students do the activity.

4. Have students tell the class which activities their partner likes and doesn't like.

5. Conduct a class poll to see which are the favorite activities and least favorite activities.

2 Listening

Class CD, Track 52

1. Have students read the directions for the activity.

2. Explain to students that they will listen to people talk about what they like to do and circle the correct answer.

3. Play the first conversation on Class CD Track 52. Make sure everyone understands why the correct answer is *a.* Play the rest of the recording. Have students do the activity. Play the recording again if necessary.

Audio script

1.

A: Do you like to eat out?

B: Yes. I eat out about once a week.

2.

A: What do you like to do in your free time?

B: I like to go dancing.

3.

A: Do you like to listen to music?

B: Sure! Don't you?

4.

A: Do you work out?

B: Yeah, I like to go to the gym about three times a week.

5.

A: Do you like to watch TV?

B: Oh, yeah. I watch TV every day.

6.

A: Do you like to go shopping?

B: Yes, I do. I go shopping every weekend.

4. Ask volunteers to read their answers for the class to check.

Answers:

1. **a.** eat out	4. **a.** work out at the gym
2. **a.** go dancing	5. **b.** watch TV
3. **b.** listen to music	6. **b.** go shopping

Notes

Explain that it is common for someone to use a negative question such as *Don't you?* when they expect agreement.

Student Book page 38

3 Grammar: Information questions; adverbs of frequency

Class CD, Track 53

1. Have students read the directions for the activity.

2. Have students look at the grammar box. Give them time to read the examples.

3. Focus students' attention on the **Memo**. Read the information with students and answer any questions.

4. Play Class CD Track 53. Have students listen. Play the recording again and have students repeat.

Audio script

A: Do you work out?

B: Yes, I do.

C: No, I don't.

A: Does Ken work out?

B: Yes, he does.

C: No, he doesn't.

A: Where do you work out?

B: At a gym.

A: Where does Ken work out?

B: At a gym.

A: How often do you work out?

B: Three times a week.

C: Three times a month.

A: How often does Ken work out?

B: Every day.

C: Never.

A: Who do you work out with?

B: With my brother.

A: When do you work out?

B: On Saturdays.

A: When does Ken work out?

B: Every day.

5. Have a student volunteer point to one of the activities on page 37 or pantomime it. Tell them to make a face that shows that they like it or don't like it. Have other students talk about the first student. For example, *Does he like to take photos? Yes, he does. How often does he take photos? Twice a week.*

Notes

1. Remind students that the intonation of Yes/No questions goes up at the end.

2. Write a frequency chart on the board that shows the difference between *every day*, *twice a week*, and *never* (other adverbs of frequency will be covered in Unit 9).

3. You may want to point out to students the difference between *every day* (an adverb) and *everyday* (an adjective as used in *Everyday activities* in Unit 4).

4 Conversation

Class CD, Track 54

Activity A

1. Focus students' attention on the photo. Ask them to say where they think the people are, what they're doing, or what the people are saying to each other.

2. Have students read the directions for the activity.

3. Play Class CD Track 54 or read the conversation twice.

   ### Audio script

   A: So, what do you do in your free time?
   B: Well, I like to go shopping.
   A: Really? Where do you go?
   B: Anywhere. Big department stores, small stores …
      I just love to go shopping!
   C: How often do you go?
   B: Oh, about once a week.
   C: Who do you go with?
   B: Usually with my sister.

4. *Group work.* Have students read the conversation, switching roles three times so that each student gets to practice each part.

5. Ask several groups to demonstrate for the class.

   Also on Student CD, Track 14

Notes

Explain to students that *Really?* is a common way to show interest in what someone has just said or to show mild surprise. *Anywhere* is another way to say *not any place special. I just love to…* is an informal way to express that you like doing something very much. *About* is used when the time or amount of something is not definite. *Usually* is another way to say *most of the time.*

Activity B

1. Have students read the directions for the activity. Explain that they will work with two partners and take turns to practice the conversation using their own information. This time they will substitute information about themselves into the conversation.

2. *Group work.* Have students do the activity.

3. Ask several groups to demonstrate for the class.

Extra

1. Have students read the directions for the activity. Have students find two new partners and practice the conversation again.

2. *Group work.* Have students do the activity. Encourage them to use the phrases in the box.

Student Book page 39

5 Communication task:
What do you like to do?

Activity A

1. Have students read the directions for the activity.

2. Focus students' attention on the chart and the examples. To check understanding, ask students questions such as, *What do you do in your free time? Where do you write that in the chart?*

3. Brainstorm other activities, other people, and other locations that students can use to fill in the chart.

4. Have students do the activity.

Activity B

1. Have students read the directions for the activity.

2. *Pair work.* Have students take turns asking each other about the answers in their charts in Activity A. Then they write their partner's answers in the chart.

3. Have several pairs demonstrate their conversation for the class.

Extra

1. Keep students in pairs and have them read the examples and the directions for the activity.

2. Focus students' attention on the **Helpful Language** note. Practice the questions by brainstorming appropriate answers with the class.

3. *Pair work.* Have students ask each other questions until they find two activities that they both like to do. Model a conversation with a student volunteer.

4. Have students tell the class about which two activities they and their partner like.

Extension

Have a class discussion about free-time activities. Ask students if there are activities that they would like to try but never have. Ask how often they would like to do those activities. Ask if there are activities that they would never want to try. Brainstorm various activities first if necessary.

Popular sports

Student Book page 40

Warm-up and review

Have a quick class poll about free-time activities. Ask students what their favorite and least favorite activities are and how often they do them. Make a chart on the board of students' answers.

6 Speaking

Class CD, Track 55

Presentation

1. Focus students' attention on the pictures and the text below each one. Explain that they will hear the terms on the CD.

2. Focus students' attention on the pictures again. Have them describe what they see.

Activity A

1. Have students read the directions for the activity.

2. Focus students' attention on the pictures and text below them. Play Class CD Track 55. Have students listen and look at the pictures. Have students repeat. Go over any words they don't know.

Audio script

volleyball	soccer	windsurfing
judo	cycling	snowboarding

3. Explain to students that they will take turns asking and answering questions about the pictures.

4. Model the sample conversation with a student volunteer.

5. *Pair work*. Have students do the activity.

6. Ask students questions about the pictures to check understanding.

Activity B

1. Have students read the directions for the activity.

2. Explain to students that they will now talk with their partner about which sports they like to play or do and which sports they like to watch.

3. Focus students' attention on the **Memo**. Read the information with students and answer any questions. Elicit other sports from students and write them on the board.

4. *Pair work*. Focus students' attention on the speech bubble. Have students do the activity.

5. Have students tell the class about their partner's favorite sports to play, do, and watch.

Extension

Focus students' attention on the photos at the top of the page again. To generate more vocabulary, ask students what special equipment or safety equipment is needed for each sport. For example, for cycling people wear a helmet, for windsurfing people wear a wet suit or a personal flotation device.

7 Listening

Class CD, Track 56

Activity A

1. Have students read the directions for the activity.

2. Explain to students that they will listen to people talk about sports and then match the speakers with the sport they talk about. Read the answer choices aloud with the class.

3. Play the first conversation on Class CD Track 56. Make sure everyone understands why the correct answer for Wang is *d*. Play the rest of the recording. Have students do the activity. Play the recording again, if necessary.

Audio script

1.
A: What do you do for exercise, Wang?
B: Well, I'm taking a judo class.
A: You can do judo?
B: Yeah, I go to class once a week.

2.
A: Do you like sports, Molly?
B: Sure. I like to play volleyball.
A: Really? How often do you play?
B: My team practices twice a week.

3.

A: What sports do you like, Jake?

B: Well, I do a lot of cycling.

A: Oh, yeah?

B: Yeah, I cycle to work every day.

4.

A: Do you like soccer, Sachi?

B: Yes, I do. I like it very much.

A: How often do you play?

B: Oh, I never play soccer. I watch it on TV.

5.

A: Do you get much exercise, Dave?

B: Not too much. But I like swimming.

A: How often do you swim?

B: Not very often. I go about once a month.

4. Ask volunteers to read their answers for the class to check.

> **Answers:**
> 1. **d.** judo
> 2. **e.** volleyball
> 3. **b.** cycling
> 4. **a.** soccer
> 5. **c.** swimming

Activity B

1. Have students read the directions for the activity.

2. Explain to students that they will listen to the CD again and check how often each person plays or does the sport.

3. Play the first conversation on Class CD Track 56 again. Make sure everyone understands why the correct answer is *Once a week*. Play the rest of the recording again and have students do the activity.

4. Ask volunteers to read their answers for the class to check.

> **Answers:**
> 1. Once a week
> 2. Twice a week
> 3. Every day
> 4. Never
> 5. Once a month

8 Grammar: Using *can* for ability

Class CD, Track 57

Activity A

1. Have students read the directions for the activity.

2. Have students look at the grammar box. Give them time to read the examples.

3. Play Class CD Track 57. Have students listen. Play the recording again and have students repeat.

Audio script

A: I can play basketball.

B: She can cook.

A: I can't play tennis.

B: She can't drive.

A: Can you paint a picture?

B: Yes I can.

C: No, I can't.

A: Can he play baseball?

B: Yes, he can.

C: No, he can't.

4. Have a student volunteer pantomime an activity and either nod or shake their head to indicate *can* or *can't*. Have students use the grammar in the box to talk about it. For example, *Can she cook? No, she can't.*

Notes

Explain to students that *can* can be used for ability.

Activity B

1. Have students read the directions for the activity.

2. Focus students' attention on the **Memo**. Read the information with students and answer any questions.

3. Focus students' attention on the list of sports and activities. Then focus their attention on the speech bubble. Model the statements and have students repeat.

5. *Pair work.* Have students do the activity.

6. Have several pairs tell the class what their partners can and can't do.

9 Conversation

Class CD, Track 58

Activity A

1. Focus students' attention on the photo. Ask them to say where the people are, what they're doing, or what they're saying to each other.

2. Have students read the directions for the activity.

3. Play Class CD Track 58 or read the conversation twice.

   Audio script

   A: What sports do you like?

   B: I like basketball and tennis.

   A: Yeah, me, too. Can you play tennis?

   B: No, I can't …, but I like to watch it on TV. What about you? What sports do you like?

   C: I like swimming and skiing.

   B: Oh, can you ski?

   C: Yes, I can. I go skiing every winter.

4. *Group work.* Have students read the conversation, switching roles three times so that each student gets to practice each part.

5. Ask several groups to demonstrate for the class.

   Also on Student CD, Track 15

Activity B

1. Have students read the directions for the activity. Explain that they will work with two partners and take turns to practice the conversation using their own information. This time they will substitute information about themselves into the conversation.

2. *Group work.* Have students do the activity.

3. Ask several groups to demonstrate for the class.

Student Book page 42

10 Communication task:
Sports survey

Activity A

1. Have students read the directions for the activity.

2. Focus students' attention on the picture at the bottom of the page. Ask students what they think the people are talking about. If necessary, draw attention to the thought bubbles and ask students what the man is thinking about (*swimming and skiing*).

3. Focus students' attention on the questions. Ask one student each question to check understanding.

4. Give students time to write two questions of their own.

5. Have students do the activity.

Activity B

1. Have students read the directions for the activity.

2. *Pair work.* Have students take turns asking each other the questions in the survey and writing their partner's answers.

3. Have students tell their partner's answers to the class. If you want, this can be conducted as a class survey, and you can tally students' answers on the board.

Student Book page 83

Check your English

To review the vocabulary and grammar from Unit 7, have students do page 83. This page can be done individually, in pairs, or as a class. It can also be assigned for homework. Alternatively, administer this page as a test at the end of the unit.

Answers:

A Vocabulary
1. baseball
2. movie
3. gym
4. beach
5. eat out
6. shopping
7. dance
8. photos
9. snowboarding
10. Internet

B Grammar
1. <u>What do you do on</u> weekends?
2. <u>Who do</u> you play with?
3. <u>Can she</u> speak English?
4. <u>Do you</u> work out alone?
5. <u>Do you like to go snowboarding</u>?
6. <u>Where does she usually</u> read?
7. <u>When can you</u> go shopping?
8. <u>When does he</u> go dancing?
9. <u>How often</u> do you eat out?
10. <u>Where do</u> you play tennis?

Life events

Components

Student Book: pages 43–48

Check your English: page 84

Class CD: tracks 59–66

Student CD: tracks 16 and 17

Target language

Vocabulary: Life events: *be born*, *start school*, *graduate*, etc.; special occasions; weekend activities

Grammar: *Be going to* future; *Wh-* questions

Themes: Life events; plans for the weekend

Student Book page 43

Warm-up and review

Put students in pairs and have them take turns asking each other about what sports they like to play or watch.

1 Speaking

Class CD, Track 59

Presentation

1. Focus students' attention on the pictures and the text below each one. Explain that they will hear the terms on the CD.

2. Focus students' attention on the pictures again. Have students describe what they see. Ask them what was the most recent life event that they were involved with.

Activity A

1. Have students read the directions for the activity.

2. Focus students' attention on the pictures and the text below them. Play Class CD Track 59. Have students listen and look at the pictures. Have students repeat. Go over any words they don't know.

   #### Audio script

be born	start school	graduate	go to college
rent an apartment		get a job	
date a boyfriend or girlfriend	fall in love	move	
celebrate a birthday		take a vacation	travel

3. Explain to students that they will take turns asking and answering questions about the events in the pictures.

4. Model the conversation with a student volunteer.

5. *Pair work.* Have students do the activity.

6. Ask students questions about the pictures to check understanding.

Activity B

1. Have students read the directions for the activity.

2. Explain to students that they will take turns asking each other which events are going to happen to them soon.

3. *Pair work.* Focus students' attention on the speech bubble. Have students do the activity.

4. Have students tell the class which events are going to happen to their partner soon.

Notes

Review time words and phrases that students can use to talk about when events happened or will happen: *last week/month/year, (three) years ago, a long time ago, a few (days) ago, in a few (days), next week/month/year*, etc.

2 Listening

Class CD, Track 60

1. Have students read the directions for the activity.

2. Explain to students that they will listen to people talk about important events and then number the pictures in the correct order.

3. Play the first conversation on Class CD Track 60. Make sure everyone understands why picture **c** is numbered *1*. Play the rest of the recording. Have students do the activity. Play the recording again if necessary.

   #### Audio script

   1. My cousin and I are going to rent an apartment.
   2. I'm so happy for my sister. She's going to graduate from college next week!
   3. My little brother is going to start school next month.
   4. My birthday is next Saturday, and I'm going to go out and celebrate with some friends.

4. Ask volunteers to read their answers for the class to check.

Answers:
a. 3   b. 4   c. 1   d. 2

Notes

Explain that in the U.S., *college* is another word for *university*. *Start school* means to begin going to elementary school.

Student Book page 44

3 Grammar:
Future with *be going to*

Class CD, Track 61

1. Have students read the directions for the activity.

2. Have students look at the grammar box. Give them time to read the examples.

3. Play Class CD Track 61. Have students listen. Play the recording again and have students repeat.

Audio script

A: Are you going to take a vacation next month?

B: Yes, I am. I'm going to take a vacation in Thailand.

C: No, I'm not.

A: Is he going to move?

B: Yes, he is. He's going to move to Hong Kong.

C: No, he isn't.

A: Are they going to rent an apartment?

B: Yes, they are. They're going to rent an apartment near the college.

C: No, they aren't.

4. Ask various students each of the questions in the grammar box. Substitute some of the events on page 43 for greater variety.

Notes

Make sure that students understand that *be going to* is used to talk about future plans (*I'm going to go to Japan next week.*). *Will* is also used to talk about the future, but it's used to indicate an intention (*I will be a better student next semester.*).

4 Conversation

Class CD, Track 62

Activity A

1. Focus students' attention on the photo. Ask them to say where they think the people are, what they're doing, or what the people are saying to each other.

2. Have students read the directions for the activity.

3. Play Class CD Track 62 or read the conversation twice.

Audio script

A: Are you going to take a vacation soon?

B: Yes, I am. I'm going to Hawaii.

A: Fabulous! Are you going to go with your parents?

B: No, my cousin is going to go with me.

A: How long are you going to stay?

B: Three weeks.

A: Wow! That's great.

B: Yeah, I'm really excited.

4. *Pair work.* Have students read the conversation, switching roles.

5. Ask several pairs to demonstrate for the class.

Also on Student CD, Track 16

Notes

Explain to students that *fabulous* is another way to say *great*.

Activity B

1. Have students read the directions for the activity. Explain that they will work with a partner and take turns to practice the conversation using their own information. This time they will substitute their own information (or use their imaginations to create made-up answers) into the conversation.

2. *Pair work.* Have students do the activity.

3. Ask several pairs to demonstrate for the class.

Extra

Put students in groups of three or four. Have them close their books and talk about a vacation they want to take. Make sure they use *be going to* to talk about the future. Brainstorm vacation vocabulary and locations first if necessary.

5 Communication task:
What are you going to do?

Activity A

1. Have students read the directions for the activity.

2. Focus students' attention on the list of future time expressions and the example sentences. To check understanding, ask students questions such as, *When are you going to graduate? When are you going to take a vacation?*

3. Have students write notes about their own future activities.

Activity B

1. Have students read the directions for the activity.

2. Focus students' attention on the sample conversation. Model it with two other students.

3. Brainstorm a list of follow-up questions with the class and write them on the board if necessary.

4. *Group work.* Have students take turns making a statement about a future plan or event. Have the other students ask questions about the plan or event.

5. Have each group report on the information they found out.

Weekend plans

Warm-up and review

Put students in pairs. Have them talk about which life events they think will happen within the next year, five years, and ten years. Make sure they use *be going to*.

6 Speaking

Class CD, Track 63

Presentation

1. Focus students' attention on the pictures and the text below each one. Explain that they will hear the terms on the CD. Elicit other weekend activities from students and write them on the board. These will be used in Activity B.

2. Focus students' attention on the pictures again. Have students describe what they see.

Activity A

1. Have students read the directions for the activity.

2. Focus students' attention on the pictures and the text below them. Play Class CD Track 63. Have students listen and look at the pictures. Have students repeat. Go over any words they don't know.

Audio script

rent a DVD	spend time with family
go away	visit a museum
study for an exam	meet friends
stay home	work

3. Explain to students that they will take turns asking and answering questions about the pictures.

4. Model the sample conversation with a student volunteer.

5. *Pair work.* Have students do the activity.

6. Ask students questions about the pictures to check understanding.

Notes

Explain that *go away* is usually used when talking about a short trip of two or three days.

Activity B

1. Have students read the directions for the activity.

2. Explain to students that they will take turns asking and telling a partner about what activities they are going to do this weekend.

3. *Pair work.* Focus students' attention on the speech bubble. Have them do the activity.

4. Have students tell the class about their partner's weekend plans.

7 Listening

Class CD, Track 64

Activity A

1. Have students read the directions for the activity.

2. Explain to students that they will listen to people talk about weekend plans and circle the correct answer.

3. Play the first conversation on Class CD Track 64. Make sure everyone understands why the correct answer is *a*. Play the rest of the recording. Have students do the activity. Play the recording again if necessary.

Audio script

1.
A: Are you going to do anything special this weekend?
B: I'm going to study for an exam.
A: Are you going to study alone?
B: No. I'm going to meet some friends. We're going to study together.

2.
A: What are your plans for the weekend?
B: I'm going to go dancing on Saturday.
A: Who are you going to go with?
B: With my new boyfriend.
A: That's nice.

3.
A: What are you and Sally going to do this weekend?
B: Nothing special. I think we're going to watch a lot of TV.
A: Are you going to watch the baseball game on Sunday?
B: Oh, yes! Sally and I love baseball!

4.
A: What are your plans for the weekend?
B: I'm going to spend some time with my family.
A: Are you going to stay home?
B: Not all weekend. We're going to eat out on Saturday.

4. Ask volunteers to read their answers for the class to check.

> **Answers:**
> 1. **a.** study for an exam   3. **a.** watch sports on TV
> 2. **b.** go dancing   4. **a.** eat out

Activity B

1. Have students read the directions for the activity.

2. Explain to students that they will listen to the CD again and check if each statement is true or false. Read the statements aloud and answer any questions about vocabulary.

3. Play the first conversation on the recording again. Make sure everyone understands why the correct answer is *False*. Play the rest of the recording again and have students do the activity.

4. Ask volunteers to read their answers for the class to check.

> **Answers:**
> 1. False   2. True   3. False   4. False

Extension

Have students listen to the CD again and write one question about each conversation. Put students in pairs and have them ask and answer the questions.

Student Book page 47

8 Grammar: *Wh-* questions with *be going to*

Class CD, Track 65

Activity A

1. Have students read the directions for the activity.

2. Have students look at the grammar box. Give them time to read the examples.

3. Play Class CD Track 65. Have students listen. Play the recording again and have students repeat.

Audio script

A: What are you going to do on Saturday?
B: I'm going to visit my parents.

A: Where are you going to be on Sunday?
B: I'm going to be at home.

A: Who are you going to be with?
B: I'm going to be with my brother.

A: When are you going to go away?
B: I'm going to go away next weekend.

A: How long are you going to study?
B: I'm going to study for two hours.

4. Ask various students each of the questions in the grammar box to check understanding.

Activity B

1. Review weekend activities as a class. Write them on the board if necessary.

2. Have students read the directions for the activity. Model the activity with a student volunteer.

3. *Pair work.* Have students take turns asking and answering questions about their partner's weekend plans.

4. Have several pairs demonstrate their conversations for the class.

9 Conversation

Class CD, Track 66

Activity A

1. Focus students' attention on the picture. Ask them to say what they think the people are doing and what the people are saying to each other. Ask them what is happening in each thought bubble (*He's reading a book. She's playing tennis.*).

2. Have students read the directions for the activity.

3. Play Class CD Track 66 or read the conversation twice.

Audio script

A: What are you going to do this weekend?
B: I'm going to play tennis on Saturday.
A: Sounds like fun! Who are you going to play with?
B: With my friend Linda. We're going to play at the tennis club.
A: Great!
B: What about you? What are your plans for the weekend?
A: Nothing much. I'm going to stay home and read.
B: Sounds boring.
A: Not really. I'm reading a very interesting book.

4. *Pair work.* Have students read the conversation, switching roles.

5. Ask several pairs to demonstrate for the class.

Also on Student CD, Track 17

Explain that *What about you?* is a common way to ask someone the same question that you just asked them. *Nothing much* is a very common, informal way to say that there is very little happening.

Activity B

1. Have students read the directions for the activity. Explain that they will work with a partner and take turns saying each part in the conversation from Activity A. This time they will substitute true information about themselves into the conversation.

2. *Pair work.* Have students do the activity.

3. Ask several pairs to demonstrate for the class.

Extra

1. Have students read the directions for the activity.

2. Focus students' attention on the words and phrases in the box. Ask students where the words and phrases can be substituted in the conversation in Activity A.

3. *Pair work.* Have students work with new partners, and have them practice the conversation again, substituting the new words and phrases into the conversation where appropriate.

4. Have several pairs demonstrate the new conversation for the class.

Student Book page 48

10 Communication task:
Find someone who…

Activity A

1. Have students read the directions for the activity.

2. Focus students' attention on the activities. Say each activity and have students raise their hands if they are going to do that activity this weekend.

Activity B

1. Have students read the directions for the activity.

2. Explain to students that they are going to ask their classmates what they are going to do this weekend, and they should try to find at least one person who will do each activity. Then they will write the person's name in the correct box.

3. Focus students' attention on the sample conversation. Model it with a student volunteer.

4. Focus attention on the follow-up text in each box. Ask volunteers to model an appropriate follow-up

question for each box. To demonstrate the activity, ask several students about a few of the activities.

5. *Class work.* Have students take turns asking each other about the activities in the survey and writing their classmates' answers.

Activity C

1. Have students read the directions for the activity.

2. Explain to students that they are going to talk about what they found out about their classmates' weekend plans. Focus students' attention on the sample and model it.

3. Demonstrate the activity. Ask one student about one of the boxes in their survey and talk about it.

4. *Group work.* Have students talk about their classmates' weekend plans.

Extension

Have students write one more question to ask another student about their weekend plans. Have them ask their question and tell the class the answer.

Student Book page 84

Check your English

To review the vocabulary and grammar from Unit 8, have students do page 84. This page can be done individually, in pairs, or as a class. It can also be assigned for homework. Alternatively, administer this page as a test at the end of the unit.

Answers:

A Vocabulary
1. graduate
2. museum
3. move
4. celebrate
5. rent
6. stay home
7. away
8. vacation

B Grammar
1. **d.** No, I'm not.
2. **f.** I'm going to study for an exam.
3. **h.** Yes, he is. He's going to make spaghetti.
4. **a.** In their apartment.
5. **e.** Next month.
6. **b.** My uncle.
7. **g.** Yes, they are.
8. **c.** Five days.

Movies

Components

Student Book: pages 49–54

Check your English: page 85

Class CD: tracks 67–74

Student CD: tracks 18 and 19

Target language

Vocabulary: Types of movies; types of TV programs

Grammar: *Wh-* questions; adverbs of frequency

Themes: Movies; TV programs

Student Book page 49

Warm-up and review

Put students in pairs and have them take turns asking each other about their plans for next weekend.

1 Speaking

Class CD, Track 67

Presentation

1. Focus students' attention on the posters and the text below each one. Explain that they will hear the terms on the CD.

2. Focus students' attention on the posters. Have students describe what they see. Ask them if they have seen any movies that are similar to the ones in the posters.

Activity A

1. Have students read the directions for the activity.

2. Focus students' attention on the posters and the text below them. Play Class CD Track 67. Have students listen and look at the posters. Have students repeat. Go over any words they don't know.

Audio script

a comedy	an action movie	an animated movie
a drama	a fantasy	a horror movie
a romance	a science fiction movie	

3. Explain to students that they will take turns asking and answering questions about the movies in the posters.

4. Model the conversation with a student volunteer.

5. *Pair work.* Have students do the activity.

6. Ask students questions about the posters to check understanding.

Activity B

1. Have students read the directions for the activity.

2. Explain to students that they will take turns telling each other what movie they want to see and what kind of movie it is. Brainstorm movie titles for each genre if necessary, and write them on the board for students' reference.

3. *Pair work.* Focus students' attention on the speech bubble. Have them do the activity.

4. Have students tell the class what movie they want to see.

2 Listening

Class CD, Track 68

1. Have students read the directions for the activity.

2. Explain to students that they will listen to people talk about movies and check which kind of movies they are talking about.

3. Play the first conversation on Class CD Track 68. Make sure everyone understands why they should have checked both *Action* and *Science fiction*. Play the rest of the recording. Have students do the activity. Play the recording again if necessary.

Audio script

1.

A: Do you like movies, Ben?

B: I *love* movies!

A: What kind of movies do you like?

B: Well, I really like action movies.

A: Hmm. Do you like science fiction movies?

B: No, not really.

2.

A: What kind of movies do you like, Liz?

B: Oh, I love horror movies. You know, Frankenstein, Dracula.

A: Really? How about action movies?

B: I like action movies, too.

3.

A: Mike, do you like action movies?

B: Not really.

A: What kind of movies do you like?

B: I like comedies.

A: Me, too. Do you like fantasy movies?

B: No, I can't stand them!

4.

A: What kind of movies do you like, Sue?

B: Well, my favorite movies are science fiction and action movies.

A: Do you like animated movies?

B: Oh, sure. I like them, too.

4. Ask volunteers to read their answers for the class to check. Ask students which types of movies were *not* checked.

Answers:

1. Action/Science fiction
2. Horror/Action
3. Action/Comedy
4. Science fiction/Action

Notes
_____

Explain that *can't stand* is an informal way to express strong dislike.

Student Book page 50

3 Grammar: *Wh-* questions

Class CD, Track 69

1. Have students read the directions for the activity.

2. Have students look at the grammar box. Give them time to read the examples.

3. Play Class CD Track 69. Have students listen. Play the recording again and have students repeat.

Audio script

A: What kind of movies do you like?

B: I like comedies.

A: What kind of movies don't you like?

B: I don't like horror movies.

A: How often do you go to the movies?

B: I go every week.

A: When do you go to the movies?

B: I go on weekends.

A: What's your favorite movie?

B: My favorite movie is *Shrek*.

A: Why do you like comedies?

B: I like comedies because they're funny.

A: Who's your favorite actor?

B: My favorite actor is Bruce Lee.

A: Who's your favorite actress?

B: My favorite actress is Audrey Hepburn.

4. Have student volunteers ask another student one of the questions in the grammar box. Tell students to give true answers.

4 Conversation

Class CD, Track 70

Activity A

1. Focus students' attention on the picture. Ask them to say where they think the people are, what they're doing, or what they're saying to each other.

2. Focus students' attention on the **Memo**. Read the information with students and answer any questions.

3. Have students read the directions for the activity.

4. Play Class CD Track 70 or read the conversation twice.

Audio script

A: How often do you go to the movies?

B: Oh, once or twice a week.

A: When do you go?

B: I usually go on weekends.

A: What kind of movies do you like?

B: My favorite movies are action movies. How about you?

A: Well, I don't really like action movies. But I like horror movies a lot.

B: Really? That's surprising.

5. *Pair work.* Have students read the conversation, switching roles.

6. Ask several pairs to demonstrate for the class.

Also on Student CD, Track 18

Activity B

1. Have students read the directions for the activity. Explain that they will work with a partner and take turns to practice the conversation using their own information. This time they will give true answers and substitute them in the conversation.

2. *Pair work.* Have students do the activity.

3. Ask several pairs to demonstrate for the class.

Extra

1. Have students read the directions for the activity.

2. Focus student's attention on the sample conversation. Put students in pairs. Have them take turns asking and answering questions about their favorite movie stars. Brainstorm reasons to like a movie star first if necessary.

Extension

Conduct a class survey to find out which actors students like best.

Student Book page 51

5 Communication task:
My favorite movie

Activity A

1. Have students read the directions for the activity.

2. Focus students' attention on the questions in each space on the movie theater marquee. Teach students vocabulary to talk about what they like about a movie such as plot, characters, setting, soundtrack, scenery, etc.

3. Have students make notes for themselves in the boxes on the marquee.

Activity B

1. Have students read the directions for the activity.

2. Focus students' attention on the speech bubble. Model talking about a favorite movie. Have a student volunteer ask a question about your movie.

3. Focus students' attention on the **Helpful Language** note. Practice the questions by brainstorming appropriate answers with the class. Brainstorm other questions that students can use to talk in groups about their favorite movie.

4. *Group work.* Have students take turns talking about their favorite movie, using their notes from Activity A. Have the other students ask questions about the movie.

5. Have each group report on the information they found out.

Extra

1. Have students read the directions for the activity.

2. Model the activity with the class. Think of a movie and give students one clue. Have students ask questions and guess the movie. Refer students to the **Helpful Language** note for questions they can ask.

3. *Group work.* Put students in small groups. Have them take turns thinking of a movie and guessing their classmates' movie.

TV programs

Student Book page 52

Warm-up and review

Put students in pairs. Have them talk about the most recent movie they've seen and if they liked it and why or why not.

6 Speaking

Class CD, Track 71

Presentation

1. Focus students' attention on the pictures and the text below each one. Explain that they will hear the terms on the CD.

2. Focus students' attention on the pictures again. Have students describe what they see. Explain to students that *sitcom* is short for *situation comedy*. Ask them to give one example of each kind of show.

Activity A

1. Have students read the directions for the activity.

2. Focus students' attention on the pictures and the text below them. Play Class CD Track 71. Have students listen and look at the pictures. Have students repeat. Go over any words they don't know.

   Audio script

news	game show
cartoon	nature program
talk show	children's program
soap opera	sports
sitcom	reality show

3. Explain to students that they will take turns asking and answering questions about the TV programs in the pictures.

4. Model the conversation with a student volunteer.

5. *Pair work.* Put students in pairs and have them do the activity.

6. Ask students questions about the pictures to check understanding.

Activity B

1. Have students read the directions for the activity.

2. Explain to students that they will now talk with their partner about what TV programs they are going to watch this weekend.

3. *Pair work.* Focus students' attention on the speech bubble. Have them do the activity.

4. Have students tell the class about their partner's answers.

7 Listening

Class CD, Track 72

Activity A

1. Have students read the directions for the activity.

2. Explain to students that they will listen to people talk about TV programs and number the kinds of programs in the order they hear them.

3. Play the first conversation on Class CD Track 72. Make sure everyone understands why *reality shows* is numbered *1*. Play the rest of the recording. Have students do the activity. Play the recording again if necessary.

   Audio script

   1.
   A: I don't like reality shows.
   B: Really? I like them very much.

   2.
   A: I like to watch game shows.
   B: Me, too. I watch them a lot!

   3.
   A: I watch a lot of cartoons on TV.
   B: Do you? I never watch them.

   4.
   A: I don't watch sitcoms very often.
   B: I don't watch them either.

   5.
   A: I like to watch news programs.
   B: Me, too. I watch the news every night.

4. Ask volunteers to read their answers for the class to check.

Activity B

1. Have students read the directions for the activity.

2. Explain to students that they will listen to the CD again and check if the second speaker likes or doesn't like to watch that kind of program.

3. Play the first conversation on Class CD Track 72 again. Make sure everyone understands why the correct answer is *Yes*. Play the rest of the recording again and have students do the activity.

4. Ask volunteers to read their answers for the class to check.

Extension

Have students listen to the CD again and write one more line for each conversation.

Student Book page 53

8 Grammar: Adverbs of frequency

Class CD, Track 73

Activity A

1. Have students read the directions for the activity.

2. Have students look at the grammar box. Give them time to read the examples.

3. Focus students' attention on the bar graph and labels. Ask volunteers to say approximately what percentage of time each adverb indicates (for example, always = 100% of the time).

3. Play Class CD Track 73. Have students listen. Play the recording again and have students repeat.

Audio script

A: Cindy always watches the news.

B: Akira usually watches cartoons.

A: Joy often watches nature programs.

B: Bob sometimes watches talk shows.

A: Ann hardly ever watches soap operas.

B: Ron never watches reality shows.

A: Do you ever watch sports on TV?

B: Yes, I always do.

A: Does Ya-ping often watch sitcoms?

B: No, she hardly ever does.

A: Does Jin-Won usually watch game shows?

B: Sometimes he does.

Activity B

1. Have students read the directions for the activity.

2. Focus students' attention on the list of activities. Read them aloud and have students repeat. Answer any questions about vocabulary.

3. Focus students' attention on the speech bubbles. Model the dialogue with a student volunteer.

4. *Pair work.* Have students take turns asking and answering questions about how often their partner does each activity.

5. Have several pairs demonstrate their conversations for the class.

9 Conversation

Class CD, Track 74

Activity A

1. Focus students' attention on the photo. Ask them to say where they think the men are, what they're doing, or what they're saying to each other.

2. Have students read the directions for the activity.

3. Play Class CD Track 74 or read the conversation twice.

Audio script

A: Do you ever watch nature programs?

B: No, I never do. I really don't like nature programs. I usually watch talk shows and sports.

A: Oh, what sports do you usually watch?

B: Well, I watch baseball and basketball a lot. Do you ever watch sports?

A: Sometimes I do. But my favorite programs are sitcoms.

B: Hmm. Do you like cartoons?

A: Oh, yeah. I really like cartoons, too.

4. *Pair work*. Have students read the conversation, switching roles.

5. Ask several pairs to demonstrate for the class.

   Also on Student CD, Track 19

Activity B

1. Have students read the directions for the activity. Explain that they will work with a partner and take turns to practice the conversation using their own information. This time they will substitute different kinds of programs and true information about themselves into the conversation.

2. *Pair work*. Have students do the activity.

3. Ask several pairs to demonstrate for the class.

Student Book page 54

10 Communication task:
What's the question?

Activity A

1. Have students read the directions for the activity.

2. Focus students' attention on the question words and the answers. To check understanding, ask a student volunteer to complete the question for the first answer.

3. Have student do the activity.

4. Have student volunteers read their answers for the class to check their answers.

> **Answers:**
>
> How often do you watch TV?
> When do you usually watch TV?
> What kind of TV shows do you like?
> What kind of TV shows don't you like?
> What is your favorite program?
> Why do you like it?

Activity B

1. Have students read the directions for the activity.

2. *Pair work*. Have students take turns asking and answering the questions from Activity A. Make sure they take notes on their partner's answers.

Activity C

1. Have students read the directions for the activity.

2. Explain to students that they are going to get together with another pair and compare answers. Focus students' attention on the sample and model it.

3. *Group work*. Have students complete the activity.

4. Have students tell the class about a group member's answers.

Extension

Conduct a class poll about the most and least popular TV shows and how often students watch TV.

Student Book page 85

Check your English

To review the vocabulary and grammar from Unit 9, have students do page 85. This page can be done individually, in pairs, or as a class. It can also be assigned for homework. Alternatively, administer this page as a test at the end of the unit.

> **Answers:**
>
> A Vocabulary
> 1. comedy
> 2. news
> 3. game show
> 4. science fiction
> 5. horror
> 6. romance
> 7. sports
> 8. nature program
>
> B Grammar
> 1. What is your favorite TV program?
> 2. Why do you like horror movies?
> 3. How often do you watch game shows?
> 4. Who is your favorite actor?
> 5. What kind of TV programs don't you like?
> 6. Do you ever watch reality shows on TV?

Health problems

Components

Student Book: pages 55–60; 76

Check your English: page 86

Class CD: tracks 75–82

Student CD: tracks 20 and 21

Target language

Vocabulary: Ailments, illnesses, and health; remedies

Grammar: *Feel* + adjective; *have* + noun; imperatives

Themes: Health problems; getting better

Student Book page 55

Warm-up and review

Put students in pairs. Tell them to imagine they have a bad cold and have to stay home and can only watch TV. Have them tell each other what they would watch on TV over a 24-hour period.

1 Speaking

Class CD, Track 75

Presentation

1. Focus students' attention on the pictures and the text below each one. Explain that they will hear the terms on the CD.

2. Focus students' attention on the pictures again. Have students describe what they see.

Activity A

1. Have students read the directions for the activity.

2. Focus students' attention on the pictures and the text below them. Play Class CD Track 75. Have students listen and look at the pictures. Have students repeat. Go over any words they don't know.

   #### Audio script

a headache	a stomachache	a toothache
a backache	an earache	a cold
a sore throat	a fever	
a cough	the flu	

3. Explain to students that they will take turns asking and answering questions about the pictures.

4. Model the conversation with a student volunteer.

5. *Pair work.* Have students do the activity.

6. Ask students questions about the pictures to check understanding.

Notes

Make sure students notice that *flu* takes a definite article (*the*), not an indefinite article (*a*). Explain that *ache* means the same as pain or discomfort.

Activity B

1. Have students read the directions for the activity.

2. Explain to students that they will take turns asking each other what is wrong with each person in the pictures at the top of the page.

3. *Pair work.* Focus students' attention on the speech bubble. Have students do the activity.

4. Have a student say what is wrong with one of the people in the pictures. Have the rest of the class point to the correct picture.

2 Listening

Class CD, Track 76

1. Have students read the directions for the activity.

2. Explain to students that they will listen to different people talk about their health problems and then circle the correct answer.

3. Play the first speaker on Class CD Track 76. Make sure everyone understands why the correct answer is *a*. Play the rest of the recording. Have students do the activity. Play the recording again if necessary.

Audio script

1. I don't feel well. I have a fever, so I'm going to see a doctor.
2. I really don't feel very well. I have a cold.
3. Oh, my tooth hurts! I'm going to see a dentist because I have a bad toothache.
4. I helped a friend move on the weekend. Now I have a backache, and I can't sleep at night.
5. I don't have a cold, but I have a sore throat. It really feels scratchy.
6. I was tired and achy. I went to see the doctor, and she said I have the flu.

4. Ask volunteers to read their answers for the class to check.

Answers:

1. **a.** a fever
2. **a.** a cold
3. **b.** a toothache
4. **b.** a backache
5. **a.** a sore throat
6. **a.** the flu

Notes

Explain that when describing physical health, *I don't feel well/very well* is correct. Explain that although *I don't feel good* is grammatically incorrect, it is commonly used in conversation in the U.S.

Student Book page 56

3 Grammar: *Feel* + adjective; *have* + noun

Class CD, Track 77

1. Have students read the directions for the activity.
2. Have students look at the grammar box. Give them time to read the examples.
3. Focus students' attention on the word box. Read each word and have students say when they would use each word (*When I have the flu, I feel terrible.*).
4. Play Class CD Track 77. Have students listen. Play the recording again and have students repeat.

Audio script

A: How do you feel?
B: I feel sick.

A: How are you?
B: I feel terrible.
   I don't feel well.

A: What's wrong?
B: I have a headache.

A: What's the matter?
B: I have a cold.
   I have the flu.

Adjectives

fine

sick

great

awful

terrific

terrible

better

worse

5. Have a student volunteer pantomime one of the ailments from page 55. Have the student do a brief role-play with another student using the language from the grammar box. Continue with other students and different ailments.

Notes

Remind students that the intonation of *Wh-* questions goes down at the end.

4 Conversation

Class CD, Track 78

Activity A

1. Focus students' attention on the picture. Ask them to say where they think the people are, and what they think the people are saying to each other.
2. Have students read the directions for the activity.
3. Play Class CD Track 78 or read the conversation twice.

Audio script

A: Hello?
B: Hi, Katy. It's Jeff.
A: Jeff? How are you?
B: Not so good. I'm afraid I can't meet you tonight.
A: Really? What's wrong?
B: I don't feel well. I have a sore throat.
A: Oh, I'm sorry to hear that. I hope you feel better soon.

4. *Pair work.* Have students read the conversation, switching roles.
5. Ask several pairs to demonstrate for the class.

Also on Student CD, Track 20

Notes

Explain to students that *I'm afraid (I can't meet you tonight)* is a common way to express regret about something. Also explain that *I'm sorry to hear that* is a common way to express sympathy and is not an apology.

Activity B

1. Have students read the directions for the activity. Explain that they will work with a partner and take turns to practice the conversation again. This time they will use their imaginations and substitute other ailments and responses into the conversation.

2. Focus students' attention on the **Helpful Language** note. Practice the responses by brainstorming what kinds of statements could come before them.

3. *Pair work.* Have partners do the activity.

4. Ask several pairs to demonstrate for the class.

Extra

1. Have students read the directions for the activity.

2. Focus students' attention on the phrases. Explain to students that they will use the phrases in a conversation like the one they had in Activity B.

3. *Pair work.* Have students do the activity.

Student Book page 57

5 Communication task:
How are you today?

1. Focus students' attention on the photo at the top of the page. Ask students what they think the women are talking about.

2. Have students read the directions for the activity.

3. Focus attention on the questions and responses in *Conversation 1*. Explain to students that the questions and responses together will make a conversation, but they are not in the correct order. Tell students that they will work with a partner to put the sentences in the correct order and practice the conversation together. Make sure they understand that sentences from one column cannot be substituted into the other column.

4. To check understanding, ask a student volunteer to say why *How are you today?* is the first line.

5. Explain to students that they will repeat the activity with the second set of sentences in *Conversation 2*.

6. *Pair work.* Have students do the activity.

7. Ask several pairs to demonstrate their conversations for the class.

Answers:

Conversation 1
Person A:
5 Do you have a fever?
7 That's too bad. I hope you feel better tomorrow.
1 How are you today?
3 What's the matter?

Person B:
4 I have a headache.
6 No, but I have a terrible backache.
8 Me, too.
2 Not so good. I feel terrible

Conversation 2
Person A:
7 Yes, and I have a stomachache.
1 How do you feel today?
5 I have a sore throat.
3 I don't feel so good.

Person B:
2 I feel fine, thanks. How about you?
8 Maybe you have the flu.
6 Do you have a cough?
4 What's wrong?

Extra

1. Keep students in pairs and have them read the directions for the activity.

2. Focus students' attention on the picture at the bottom of the page. Ask students what they think the people are doing.

3. Model the activity with a student volunteer. Pretend to have an ailment and have the student ask you how you are and guess what your ailment is.

4. *Pair work.* Have students do the activity.

Getting better

Warm-up and review

Have students use their dictionaries to look up symptoms of different ailments such as allergy, stuffy nose, sneeze, rash, etc. Have them ask each other if they have ever had these symptoms.

6 Speaking

Class CD, Track 79

Presentation

1. Focus students' attention on the pictures and the text below each one. Explain that they will hear the terms on the CD.

2. Focus students' attention on the pictures again. Have students describe what they see.

Activity A

1. Have students read the directions for the activity.

2. Focus students' attention on the pictures and the text below them. Play Class CD Track 79. Have students listen and look at the pictures. Have students repeat. Go over any words they don't know.

    Audio script

take some aspirin	take some cough syrup
take a hot bath	stay in bed
see a dentist	get some exercise
see a doctor	drink some tea

3. Explain to students that they will take turns asking and answering questions about the pictures.

4. Model the sample conversation with a student volunteer.

5. *Pair work*. Put students in pairs and have them do the activity.

6. Ask students questions about the pictures to check understanding.

Activity B

1. Have students read the directions for the activity.

2. Explain to students that they will take turns asking and telling a partner about what they do when they feel ill.

3. *Pair work*. Focus students' attention on the speech bubble. Have them do the activity.

4. Have students tell the class about their partner's favorite remedies.

7 Listening

Class CD, Track 80

Activity A

1. Have students read the directions for the activity.

2. Explain to students that they will listen to people talk about health problems and circle the correct answer.

3. Play the first conversation on Class CD Track 80. Make sure everyone understands why the correct answer is *b*. Play the rest of the recording. Have students do the activity. Play the recording again if necessary.

    Audio script

    1.
    A: You look terrible. What's wrong?
    B: I have a really bad headache.
    A: That's too bad. Here. Take some aspirin.
    B: Gee, thanks!

    2.
    A: What's the matter with you? Do you feel sick?
    B: No, but I feel really tired. I can't sleep at night. What can I do?
    A: Take a hot bath. Then you can relax and go to sleep.

    3.
    A: Do you ever get a sore throat?
    B: No, but I get a lot of colds. I have a cold right now.
    A: I'm sorry to hear that. Have a cup of tea.

4. Ask volunteers to read their answers for the class to check.

> **Answers:**
> 1. **b.** headache   2. **a.** sleep   3. **a.** colds

Activity B

1. Have students read the directions for the activity.

2. Explain to students that they will listen to the CD again. This time they will listen for the remedy that the friends suggest.

3. Play the first conversation on Class CD Track 80 again. Make sure everyone understands why the correct answer is *b*. Play the rest of the recording again and have students do the activity.

4. Ask volunteers to read their answers for the class to check.

> **Answers:**
> 1. **b.** take some aspirin
> 2. **b.** take a hot bath
> 3. **c.** drink some tea

Student Book page 59

8 Grammar: Imperatives

Class CD, Track 81

Activity A

1. Have students read the directions for the activity.

2. Have students look at the grammar box. Give them time to read the examples.

3. Play Class CD Track 81. Have students listen. Play the recording again and have students repeat.

   Audio script

   A: Stay home and relax.
   B: Don't go to school.
   A: Drink lots of water.
   B: Don't eat desserts.
   A: Go to bed early.
   B: Don't work too hard.

4. Have a student volunteer act out an illness. Have another student suggest what to do to feel better. Continue with other students.

Notes

Explain to students that the imperative form of a verb is often used to tell someone to do something or give strong advice.

Activity B

1. Have students read the directions for the activity.

---

2. Focus attention on the list of remedies. Explain to students that they will use the phrases to complete the conversations. Brainstorm other possible remedies and write them on the board if necessary.

3. *Pair work.* Tell students to work together to complete the conversations and then to practice the conversations.

4. Have several pairs demonstrate their conversations for the class.

9 Conversation

Class CD, Track 82

Activity A

1. Focus students' attention on the photo. Ask them to say who they think the people are (*doctor and patient*), where they are, and what they think the people are saying to each other.

2. Have students read the directions for the activity.

3. Play Class CD Track 82 or read the conversation twice.

   Audio script

   A: I don't feel so good, doctor.
   B: What's wrong?
   A: I have a sore throat and a cough.
   B: Do you have a fever?
   A: No, but I feel very tired.
   B: It sounds like you have a bad cold. Take this cough syrup and get some rest. Drink lots of water. And don't work too hard.
   A: OK, doctor.
   B: And don't worry. You're going to be fine!

4. *Pair work.* Have students read the conversation, switching roles.

5. Ask several pairs to demonstrate for the class.

   Also on Student CD, Track 21

Notes

Explain to students that *I don't feel so good* is common usage in the U.S., and is not considered incorrect in conversation.

Activity B

1. Have students read the directions for the activity. Explain that they will work with a partner and take turns saying each part in the conversation from Activity A. This time they will substitute other illnesses and remedies into the conversation.

2. *Pair work.* Have students do the activity.

3. Ask several pairs to demonstrate for the class.

10 Communication task:
Things you can do for a...

Activity A

1. Put students in pairs and have them decide who will be Student A and who will be Student B. Have Student A look at page 60 and Student B look at page 76. Have students read the directions for the activity.

2. Focus students' attention on the chart. To check understanding, ask students, *What can you do if you get a lot of colds?*

3. *Pair work.* Have students do the activity.

Activity B

1. Have students read the directions for the activity.

2. *Group work.* Put pairs in groups of four. Tell them to compare their charts and fill in the chart with any new remedies.

3. Have students tell their group's remedies to the class.

Extension

Have a class discussion about remedies for different illnesses. Ask students if they know of any unusual or old-fashioned remedies. Explain what the hiccups are. Ask students for their favorite remedy for stopping the hiccups.

Check your English

To review the vocabulary and grammar from Unit 10, have students do page 86. This page can be done individually, in pairs, or as a class. It can also be assigned for homework. Alternatively, administer this page as a test at the end of the unit.

Answers:

A Vocabulary
1. cough syrup
2. flu
3. stomachache
4. cold
5. terrific
6. aspirin
7. exercise
8. terrible

B Grammar
Doctor: How do you <u>feel</u> today?
Patient: I feel <u>awful</u>.
Doctor: What's the matter?
Patient: I <u>have</u> a really bad headache.
Doctor: Do you have a <u>fever</u>?
Patient: Yes, and I'm very tired.
Doctor: Maybe you have the flu. <u>Go</u> home and <u>get</u> some rest. <u>Take</u> these pills. And <u>don't</u> go to work.

<table>
<tr><td>

Components

Student Book: pages 61–66

Check your English: page 87

Class CD: tracks 83–90

Student CD: tracks 22 and 23

</td><td>

Target language

Vocabulary: Vacation locations and activities; life events in the past; time markers

Grammar: Simple past: questions and statements; *to be*: simple past

Themes: On vacation; past events

</td></tr>
</table>

Student Book page 61

Warm-up and review

Write a list of remedies and a list of ailments on the board in random order. Have students say which remedies could be for which ailment. Put students in pairs and have them do a short role-play of someone with a few ailments talking to a doctor.

1 Speaking

Class CD, Track 83

Presentation

1. Focus students' attention on the pictures and the text below each one. Explain that they will hear the terms on the CD.

2. Focus students' attention on the pictures again. Have students describe what they see.

Activity A

1. Have students read the directions for the activity.

2. Focus students' attention on the pictures and the text below them. Play Class CD Track 83. Have students listen and look at the pictures. Have students repeat. Go over any words they don't know.

Audio script

went to Guam	arrived on Tuesday	felt excited
rented a car	studied lots of maps	
visited Tarzan Falls	went windsurfing	
ate in restaurants	bought souvenirs	took photos
had a good time	came home	

3. Explain to students that they will take turns asking and answering questions about the vacation in the pictures.

4. Model the conversation with a student volunteer.

5. *Pair work.* Have students do the activity.

6. Ask students questions about the pictures to check understanding.

Notes

Guam, a small island in the Pacific Ocean (541 square km), has a population of just over 170,000 people, about 45 percent of whom are native Chamorros. It's a popular tourist destination, attracting more than 1 million visitors a year. Because of its tropical climate, Guam is known for outdoor sports such as windsurfing, diving, and snorkeling. Two of the sites pictured in the Student Book are Tarzan Falls and Latte Park.

Tarzan Falls are located in southern Guam and range in height from 2.4 to 15 m. They're popular with hikers who reach the falls by foot and swim in the pools at the base of the falls.

Latte Park (shown in the picture labeled *took photos*), in the capital of Hagatna, is named for the large stone pillars there. They were moved to Hagatna from a village and date back to 500 A.D. Ancient Chamorro houses were built on these types of pillars.

Activity B

1. Have students read the directions for the activity.

2. Explain to students that they will take turns telling each other about what they did on a vacation that they took.

3. *Pair work.* Focus students' attention on the speech bubble. Have students do the activity.

4. Have students tell the class about their partner's vacation.

2 Listening

Class CD, Track 84

1. Have students read the directions for the activity.

2. Explain to students that they will listen to people talking about vacations and check the activities that they did on vacation. Read the answer choices aloud and answer any questions about vocabulary. Make sure students understand that there is one extra activity that won't be mentioned.

3. Play the first conversation on Class CD Track 84. Make sure everyone understands why the correct answer is *Went to Thailand*. Play the rest of the recording. Have students do the activity. Play the recording again if necessary.

Audio script

1.

A: Did you have a good vacation?

B: I had a great vacation!

A: Where did you go?

B: I went to Thailand.

2.

A: Did you have a good time on your vacation?

B: Not bad.

A: Where did you go?

B: Oh, I didn't go away. I just stayed home and relaxed.

3.

A: When did you get back from vacation?

B: Last week.

A: Did you go to the beach?

B: No, not this time. I visited relatives in California.

4.

A: What did you do on your vacation?

B: I went skiing.

A: Did you have a good time?

B: Yeah. Terrific!

4. Ask volunteers to read their answers for the class to check.

Answers:

1. Went to Thailand	3. Visited relatives
2. Stayed home	4. Went skiing

Notes

Explain that *not bad* is an informal way to express that something was good, but not great. *Go away*, in the context of vacation, means to have a vacation away from home. *Get back* means the same as *return home*. *Relatives* is a general term for family members.

Extension

Play Class CD Track 84 again. Have students say if each speaker said if they enjoyed their vacation and what words they used to describe it.

3 Grammar: Simple past tense— questions and statements

Class CD, Track 85

1. Have students read the directions for the activity.

2. Have students look at the grammar box. Give them time to read the examples.

3. Focus students' attention on the **Memo**. Read the information with students and answer any questions.

4. Play Class CD Track 85. Have students listen. Play the recording again and have students repeat.

Audio script

A: Did you go to Vietnam?

B: No, I didn't go to Vietnam.

A: Where did you go?

B: I went to Hong Kong.

A: Who did you go with?

B: I went with my cousin.

A: What did you do?

B: I went to a karaoke club.

A: What did you see?

B: I saw the Tin Hau Temple.

A: What did you visit?

B: I visited the Museum of Art.

A: When did you come home?

B: We came home last Sunday.

A: Did you enjoy your vacation?

B: Yes, I did.

A: Did you have any problems?

B: No, I didn't.

5. Say one of the verbs from the grammar box in the present tense and have students say it in the past tense.

6. Brainstorm other verbs that can be used to describe a vacation. Write the present and past tense forms on the board. Have students make past tense sentences using the verbs on the board (*Did you eat anything unusual?*).

Notes

1. Review regular and irregular verbs with students. Explain that regular verbs end in *-ed* and irregular verbs have different spellings that must be memorized.

2. Make sure students pay special attention to how the verb is in the present tense form in the question, but in the past tense form in the answer.

3. Tin Hau Temple, a popular destination in Hong Kong, probably dates from the 18th century. It is dedicated to Tin Hau, goddess of the sea and patron of fishermen and sailors.

4 Conversation

Class CD, Track 86

Activity A

1. Focus students' attention on the picture. Ask them to say where they think the people are and what they think the people are talking about. Ask them to describe what's happening in the speech bubbles.

2. Have students read the directions for the activity.

3. Play Class CD Track 86 or read the conversation twice.

   Audio script

   A: Where did you go on vacation?

   B: I went to San Francisco with some friends.

   A: That sounds like fun. How long did you stay?

   B: Just one week. How about you? Did you go away?

   A: No, I didn't. I stayed home.

   B: Really? What did you do?

   A: Nothing much—I slept late. I visited friends. I went out to eat …

   B: Sounds like you had fun, too.

4. *Pair work.* Have students read the conversation, switching roles.

5. Ask several pairs to demonstrate for the class.

   Also on Student Class CD, Track 22

Notes

Explain that *Sounds like fun* is an informal way to say that something seems like it is fun.

Activity B

1. Have students read the directions for the activity. Explain that they will work with a partner and take turns saying each part in the conversation from Activity A. This time they will substitute other vacations and activities into the conversation.

2. Remind students that they can use their imagination if they don't want to talk about a real vacation. Brainstorm ideas as a class if necessary.

3. *Pair work.* Have students do the activity.

4. Ask several pairs to demonstrate for the class.

Extra

1. Have students read the directions for the activity. Focus attention on the list of activities. Brainstorm other activities as a class.

2. Have students make a list of three things they did on their last vacation and a list of three things they didn't do.

3. *Pair work.* Have students tell their partner about their vacation.

Student Book page 63

5 Communication task:
My last vacation

Activity A

1. Have students read the directions for the activity.

2. Focus students' attention on the questions. Tell students that they will write two more questions.

3. To check understanding, ask the questions to several students. Brainstorm any additional vocabulary students need to describe their vacation.

4. Have students do the activity.

Activity B

1. Have students read the directions for the activity. Then have them read the sample conversation.

2. Focus students' attention on the **Helpful Language** note. To check understanding, brainstorm possible answers to each question.

3. *Group work.* Put students in groups of three or four. Have them take turns asking each other about their last vacation.

Extension

Conduct a class survey about vacations. Discuss questions such as:

> *What is the most common vacation location that the class has been to?*

> *What is the most popular vacation activity?*

> *Which vacation would most of the class like to go on in the future?*

Past events

Warm-up and review

On the board, write several verbs that can be used to describe a vacation. Put students in pairs and have them use the verbs on the board to tell each other about their last vacation.

6 Speaking

Class CD, Track 87

Presentation

1. Focus students' attention on the pictures and the text below each one. Explain that they will hear the sentences on the CD.

2. Focus students' attention on the pictures again. Have students describe what they see.

Activity A

1. Have students read the directions for the activity.

2. Focus students' attention on the pictures and text below them. Play Class CD Track 87. Have students listen and look at the pictures. Have students repeat. Go over any words they don't know.

   Audio script

   Hyun-ki was born in Pusan, Korea.
   His family moved to Seoul when he was three.
   He grew up in Seoul.
   He started school when he was five.
   He attended high school in Seoul.
   He graduated from high school two years ago.
   He took a trip to Australia in 2006.
   He entered college when he was 18.

3. Explain to students that they will take turns asking and answering questions about the person in the pictures.

4. Model the sample conversation with a student volunteer.

5. *Pair work.* Put students in pairs and have them do the activity.

6. Ask students questions about the pictures to check understanding.

Activity B

1. Have students read the directions for the activity.

2. Explain to students that they will now tell their partner three or more things about their past.

3. *Pair work.* Focus students' attention on the speech bubble. Have students do the activity.

4. Have students tell the class about past events in their partner's life.

Extension

Focus students' attention on the pictures at the top of the page. Ask them to make a question for each of the sentences.

7 Listening

Class CD, Track 88

Activity A

1. Have students read the directions for the activity.

2. Explain to students that they will listen to people talk about past events in their lives and number the pictures in the correct order.

3. Play the first conversation on Class CD Track 88. Make sure everyone understands why picture **d** is numbered *1*. Play the rest of the recording. Have students do the activity. Play the recording again if necessary.

   Audio script

   1.
   A: So, what's new with you?
   B: My brother and I took a trip to Hong Kong.
   A: Sounds great! When did you go?
   B: Last month.

   2.
   A: And this is a picture of me when I started school.
   B: You look really cute. How old were you?
   A: I was very young. I was only four.

   3.
   A: I heard you rented an apartment.
   B: Yeah. It's really nice.
   A: When are you going to move in?
   B: I moved in yesterday.
   A: Well, good luck!

4.

A: Did you go to State University?
B: Yeah, I did.
A: I went there, too. When did you graduate?
B: Three years ago.
A: Me, too.

4. Ask volunteers to read their answers for the class to check.

> **Answers:**
>
> **a.** 3   **b.** 4   **c.** 2   **d.** 1

Activity B

1. Have students read the directions for the activity.

2. Explain to students that they will listen to the CD again and circle the correct information under each picture. Read the answer choices aloud and answer any questions about vocabulary.

3. Play the first conversation on Class CD Track 88 again. Make sure everyone understands why the correct answer is *b*. Play the rest of the recording again and have students do the activity.

4. Ask volunteers to read their answers for the class to check.

> **Answers:**
>
> **a.** b. yesterday   **c.** b. when she was four
> **b.** b. three years ago   **d.** b. last month

Student Book page 65

8 Grammar:
Simple past tense of *be*

Class CD, Track 89

Activity A

1. Have students read the directions for the activity.

2. Have students look at the grammar box. Give them time to read the examples.

3. Focus students' attention on the **Memo**. Read the information with students and answer any questions.

4. Play Class CD Track 89. Have students listen. Play the recording again and have students repeat.

Audio script

A: When were you born?
B: I was born in 1987.

A: Were you born in the U.S.?
B: No, I wasn't.
A: Where were you born?
B: I was born in Japan.
A: Was your sister born in Japan?
B: Yes, she was.
A: What city was she born in?
B: She was born in Osaka.
A: Were your parents born in Osaka?
B: No, they weren't.
A: Where were they born?
B: They were born in Nagoya.
A: Were your grandparents from Nagoya?
B: Yes, they were.
A: Was your grandfather Japanese?
B: Yes, he was.

5. Ask various students each of the questions in the grammar box to check understanding.

Activity B

1. Have students read the directions for the activity.

2. *Pair work.* Have students take turns asking each other about life events in the past.

3. Have students tell the class about their partner's answers.

9 Conversation

Class CD, Track 90

Activity A

1. Focus students' attention on the picture. Ask students what they think the women are talking about.

2. Have students read the directions for the activity.

3. Play Class CD Track 90 or read the conversation twice.

Audio script

A: Do you remember your first boyfriend, Emi?
B: Oh, sure. I remember him. He was really cute!
A: Where was he from?
B: He was from Australia. We were so in love!
A: No kidding? How old were you?
B: I was 15. And he was about 16.
A: What was his name?
B: You know what? I can't remember!

4. *Pair work.* Have students read the conversation, switching roles.

5. Ask several pairs to demonstrate for the class.

Also on Student Class CD, Track 23

Remind students that *cute* is an informal way to say that a young man or young woman is attractive. *So* is another way to say *very. No kidding?* is an informal way to express surprise at something someone has just said.

Activity B

1. Have students read the directions for the activity. Explain that they will work with a partner and take turns to practice the conversation using their own information. This time they will talk about their best friend in school and substitute true responses.

2. *Pair work.* Have partners do the activity.

3. Ask several pairs to demonstrate for the class.

Extra

1. Have students read the directions for the activity. Explain to students that childhood is the period of time from when someone is about four years old until they are about twelve years old. Give students time to think of an important person from their past.

2. *Pair work.* Students take turns asking each other about the important person from their past.

3. Have students tell the class about their partner's answers.

Student Book page 66

10 Communication task:
A happy event in my life

Activity A

1. Have students read the directions for the activity.

2. Focus students' attention on the pictures around the chart. Have students say what happy past event each picture could symbolize.

3. Focus students' attention on the questions in the chart. To check understanding, have several students ask you the questions and write your answers on the board.

4. Explain to students that they will think of a happy event in the past, either the recent past or long ago. Then they will answer the questions and write their answers in the *Your event* column in the chart.

5. Have students do the activity on their own.

Activity B

1. Have students read the directions for the activity.

2. Focus students' attention on the **Helpful Language** note. Brainstorm questions that use the language in the note.

3. *Pair work.* Have students take turns asking each other about their happy event. Tell them to take notes on their partner's answers and write them in the chart.

Activity C

1. Have students read the directions for the activity.

2. *Class activity.* Have students tell the class about their partner's happy event.

Extension

Have students repeat Activities A, B, and C. This time have them use their imaginations to think of a funny or unusual happy event.

Student Book page 87

Check your English

To review the vocabulary and grammar from Unit 11, have students do page 87. This page can be done individually, in pairs, or as a class. It can also be assigned for homework. Alternatively, administer this page as a test at the end of the unit.

Answers:

A Vocabulary
1. was born
2. moved
3. grew up
4. entered
5. studied
6. graduated
7. took a trip

B Grammar
Akira and Ben <u>took</u> (take) a trip to San Francisco. They <u>arrived</u> (arrive) in the city on Friday. They <u>were</u> (be) very excited. They <u>stayed</u> (stay) for the weekend. They <u>had</u> (have) a great time. They <u>ate</u> (eat) Chinese food in Chinatown. They <u>attended</u> (attend) a basketball game, and they <u>bought</u> (buy) some souvenirs. They <u>felt</u> (feel) very tired when they <u>came</u> (come) home.

Telephone language  Unit

Student Book page 67

Components

Student Book: pages 67–72

Check your English: page 88

Class CD: tracks 91–98

Student CD: tracks 24 and 25

Target language

Vocabulary: Telephone language; taking and leaving messages; chores

Grammar: Requests with *can* and *could*; object pronouns; *would*; verb + *to*

Themes: Telephone language; things to do

Warm-up and review

Put students in pairs and have them take turns asking each other about what they did on their last birthday.

1 Speaking

Class CD, Track 91

Presentation

1. Focus students' attention on the pictures, the speech bubbles, and the text below each picture. Explain that they will hear the conversations and terms on the CD.

2. Explain to students that you can leave a message on an answering machine, ask a person to write the message, or key a text message on a cell phone and send it to someone else's cell phone. Ask students how they leave messages.

Activity A

1. Have students read the directions for the activity.

2. Focus students' attention on the pictures and the text below them. Play Class CD Track 91. Have students listen and look at the pictures. Have students repeat. Go over any words they don't know.

Audio script

Leaving messages

answering machine

A: Hello, this is Yu-mi. I'm sorry, but I can't come to the phone right now. Please leave a message after the beep.

leave a message

B: Hi, Yu-mi. This is Mark. I have a question about the homework. Can you call me? My number is 918-555-7023. Bye.

text message

Taking messages

make a phone call

A: Hi. Is Dave there?

B: Who's calling, please?

introduce yourself

A: This is Miki Ono.

B: Dave's not here. But he's going to be home any minute now.

take a message

B: Do you want to leave a message?

A: Yes. Please tell him I called.

3. Focus attention on the speech bubbles in the *Leaving messages* row. Read them aloud. Answer any questions about vocabulary.

4. Focus attention on the speech bubbles in the *Taking messages* row. Read them aloud. Answer any questions about vocabulary.

5. Explain to students that they will take turns asking and answering questions about the pictures.

6. Model the sample conversation with a student volunteer.

7. *Pair work.* Have students do the activity.

8. Ask students questions about the pictures to check understanding.

Activity B

1. Have students read the directions for the activity.

2. Explain to students that they will take turns pretending to call and leave a message for their partner.

3. *Pair work.* Focus students' attention on the speech bubbles. Have them do the activity.

4. Have students tell the class their partner's message.

2 Listening

Class CD, Track 92

1. Have students read the directions for the activity.

2. Explain to students that they will listen to phone calls. One speaker calls to speak to someone, and another speaker says why the person cannot come to the phone. Students will circle the correct answer for the question, *Why can't the people come to the phone?* Read the answer choices aloud and answer any questions about vocabulary.

3. Play the first conversation on Class CD Track 92. Make sure everyone understands why the correct answer is *a*. Play the rest of the recording. Have students do the activity. Play the recording again if necessary.

Audio script

1.

A: Hello?

B: Hello. Can I please speak to Ali?

A: I'm sorry. He can't come to the phone right now. He's in the shower.

2.

A: Hello.

B: Hello. Could I speak to Nora, please?

A: I'm sorry, but she's not here right now. She's away on a trip. Do you want to leave a message?

3.

A: Hello?

B: Hello. Can I speak to Ken, please?

A: Oh, I'm sorry, but he can't come to the phone right now. He's sleeping.

4.

A: Hello.

B: Hello. This is Jiro Tanaka. Can I please speak to Jodi?

A: I'm sorry, but she's not at home right now. Do you want to leave a message?

4. Ask volunteers to read their answers for the class to check.

> **Answers:**
> 1. **a.** He's in the shower.
> 2. **b.** She's on a trip
> 3. **a.** He's sleeping.
> 4. **b.** She's not at home.

Notes

Explain that *Can I speak to…* and *Could I speak to…* mean the same thing.

Student Book page 68

3 Grammar: *Can* and *could* in requests; object pronouns

Class CD, Track 93

1. Have students read the directions for the activity.

2. Have students look at the grammar box. Give them time to read the examples.

3. Focus attention on the word box on the right. Remind students that a pronoun is a word that can be substituted for another noun. Review with students that subject pronouns are the subject in a sentence and object pronouns are the object in a sentence.

4. Play Class CD Track 93. Have students listen. Play the recording again and have students repeat.

Audio script

Can and *could* in requests

A: Can I speak to Justin?

B: He's in the shower. Can you call back later?

A: Could I please speak to Emma?

B: She's in class. Can I take a message?

Object pronouns

A: Please give me the number. I don't have it.

B: Please give her a message. Ask her to call me.

A: You can call him at work. I'll give him the message.

B: Please ask them to call us.

5. Ask various students each of the questions in the grammar box.

4 Conversation

Class CD, Track 94

Activity A

1. Focus students' attention on the photos. Ask them to say where they think the people are, what the people are doing, or what the people are saying to each other.

2. Have students read the directions for the activity.

3. Play Class CD Track 94 or read the conversation twice.

Audio script

A: Hello.

B: Hi, Julie. It's Ted. Can I please speak to Michelle?

A: Oh, hi, Ted. Michelle isn't here right now. She's at the library.

B: Well, could you please take a message?

A: Sure. What's the message?

B: Ask her to call me at my brother's house.

A: OK. Just give me the number.

B: It's 314-555-0859.

A: 314-555-0859. Right?

B: Yes, that's it. Thanks a lot, Julie.

A: OK. Bye.

4. *Pair work.* Have students read the conversation, switching roles.

5. Ask several pairs to demonstrate for the class.

Also on Student CD, Track 24

Notes

Explain that *Right?* is an informal way to ask *Is that correct? Thanks a lot* is an informal way to say *Thank you very much. Bye* is an informal way to say *good-bye.*

Activity B

1. Have students read the directions for the activity. Explain that they will work with a partner and take turns saying each part in the conversation from Activity A. This time they will substitute different names and information.

2. *Pair work.* Have students do the activity.

3. Ask several pairs to demonstrate for the class.

Extra

Have students change partners and practice the conversation again. Encourage students to think of funny or unusual messages.

Extension

Put students in pairs and have them sit back-to-back. Have them role-play leaving messages and taking messages.

Student Book page 69

5 Communication task:
On the phone

1. Have students read the directions for the activity.

2. Focus students' attention on the picture. Ask them what they think the people are talking about.

3. Focus students' attention on the two columns of questions and responses. Explain to students that the questions and responses together will make

a telephone conversation, but they are not in the correct order. Tell students that they will work with a partner to put the sentences in the correct order and then practice the conversation. Make sure they understand that sentences from one column cannot be substituted into the other column.

4. To check understanding, ask a student volunteer why *Hello* is the first line.

5. *Pair work.* Have students do the activity.

Answers:

Person A:

9   You're welcome. Good-bye.

1   Hello.

7   OK. I'll give him the message.

5   Sure. What's the phone number?

3   Oh, hi, Sally. I'm sorry. Greg's not at home right now. Can I take a message?

Person B:

6   It's 212-555-0859.

8   Thank you.

10   Good-bye.

4   Yes, please. Could you ask him to call me at work?

2   Hi, Jeff. This is Sally. Can I speak to Greg, please?

Activity B

1. Have students read the directions for the activity.

2. Focus students' attention on the list of directions. Answer any questions about what to do in each step.

3. Model the activity with a student volunteer.

4. *Pair work.* Have students take turns being A and B in the conversation.

5. Have several pairs demonstrate their conversation for the class.

Things to do

Student Book page 70

Warm-up and review

Put students in pairs and have them practice leaving a message and taking a message. Put sample messages on the board as a guide if necessary.

6 Speaking

Class CD, Track 95

Presentation

1. Focus students' attention on the pictures and the text below each one. Explain that they will hear the terms on the CD.

2. Focus students' attention on the pictures again. Ask them to describe what they see. Brainstorm other common activities that students can use in Activity B.

Activity A

1. Have students read the directions for the activity.

2. Focus students' attention on the pictures and the text below them. Play Class CD Track 95. Have students listen and look at the pictures. Have students repeat. Go over any words they don't know.

   #### Audio script

take an exam	fix a bicycle
baby-sit	do the laundry
clean the apartment	do homework
go to class	go to bed early

3. Explain to students that they will take turns asking and answering questions about the activities in the pictures.

4. Model the sample conversation with a student volunteer.

5. *Pair work.* Have students do the activity.

6. Ask students questions about the pictures to check understanding.

Activity B

1. Have students read the directions for the activity.

2. Explain to students that they will now talk with their partner about what they have to do this weekend.

3. *Pair work.* Focus students' attention on the speech bubble. Have students do the activity.

4. Have students tell the class about what their partner has to do this weekend.

7 Listening

Class CD, Track 96

Activity A

1. Have students read the directions for the activity.

2. Explain to students that they will listen to people invite other people to go places and check if they can go or can't go.

3. Play the first conversation on Class CD Track 96. Make sure everyone understands why the correct answer is *Can't go*. Play the rest of the recording. Have students do the activity. Play the recording again if necessary.

   #### Audio script

   1.

   A: Jenny, this is Ben. Do you want to go to the movies with me tomorrow night?

   B: Oh, Ben. I'd love to, but I can't. I have to do homework.

   2.

   A: Say, Matt. I have an extra ticket for the baseball game on Friday. Do you want to go with me?

   B: Sure! I'd love to. What time does it start?

   3.

   A: Do you want to go shopping with me on Saturday, Carol?

   B: Gee, I'd really like to, but I can't. I have to clean my apartment.

   4.

   A: Do you want to play tennis on Sunday morning, Ethan?

   B: Sure! Where do you usually play?

4. Ask volunteers to read their answers for the class to check.

Answers:

1. Can't go
2. Can go
3. Can't go
4. Can go

Notes

Explain that *Say…* is used to get someone's attention or to change the subject in a conversation. *Sure!* can be used to say *yes* enthusiastically. *Gee* is an interjection used to express many things such as regret or surprise.

Activity B

1. Have students read the directions for the activity.

2. Explain to students that they will listen to the CD again and, for the people who can't go, write the reason they give.

3. Play the first conversation on the recording again. Make sure everyone understands that the answer is *She has to do homework.* Play the rest of the recording and have students do the activity.

4. Ask volunteers to read their answers for the class to check.

Answers:

1. She has to do homework.
3. She has to clean her apartment.

Student Book page 71

8 Grammar: *Would;* verb + *to*

Class CD, Track 97

Activity A

1. Have students read the directions for the activity.

2. Have students look at the grammar box. Give them time to read the examples.

3. Focus students' attention on the **Memo**. Read the information with students and answer any questions.

4. Play Class CD Track 97. Have students listen. Play the recording again and have students repeat.

Audio script

A: Would you like to see a movie tomorrow night?
B: Yes, I'd love to.

A: Would you like to go out to dinner with me tonight?
B: I'd like to, but I can't. I have to work late.
A: Do you want to go to a concert on Friday night?
B: I can't. I need to baby-sit my little sister.
A: Do you want to go to the soccer game on Saturday?
B: Sorry. I really want to, but I can't. I have to go to the dentist.

5. Ask a student to do something (*Do you want to go to a movie?*). Nod or shake your head to elicit an affirmative or negative answer. Have the student answer. Continue with other invitations and different students.

Activity B

1. Have students read the directions for the activity. Tell students that sometimes more than one answer is possible. Read the sample answers aloud. Ask students if any other answers are possible (*have to* can also be *need to*).

2. *Pair work.* Have students work together to complete the conversations and then practice them.

3. Have several pairs say one of the conversations for the class.

Answers:

1. A: <u>Would</u> you like <u>to</u> go swimming on Saturday?
   B: I'm sorry, I <u>can't</u>. I <u>have to</u> go to the dentist.
2. A: <u>Do</u> you want <u>to</u> go shopping tomorrow?
   B: I'd <u>love to (like to)</u>, but I can't. I <u>have to (need to)</u> work late.
3. A: Would you <u>like</u> to see a play on Sunday?
   B: I can't. I <u>have to</u> baby-sit.
4. A: Do you <u>want to</u> go to a party on Friday night?
   B: Yes, I'd <u>love to</u>!

9 Conversation

Class CD, Track 98

Activity A

1. Focus students' attention on the pictures. Ask them to say where they think the people are and what they think the people are talking about.

2. Have students read the directions for the activity.

3. Play Class CD Track 98 or read the conversation twice.

A: Hello?

B: Hello, Laura? This is In-sook.

A: In-sook! How are you?

B: I'm fine. How are you?

A: Great!

B: Listen. Would you like to come over for dinner on Friday? I'm making Korean food.

A: I'd love to. What time do you want me to come?

B: Oh, about 7:00. Do you have my address?

A: No, I don't. What is it?

B: It's 238 Park Street.

A: 238 Park Street. OK. See you on Friday!

4. *Pair work*. Have students read the conversation, switching roles.

5. Ask several pairs to demonstrate for the class.

   Also on Student CD, Track 25

Activity B

1. Have students read the directions for the activity. Explain that they will work with a partner and take turns to practice the conversation. This time they will substitute different names and information.

2. *Pair work*. Have partners do the activity.

3. Ask several pairs to demonstrate for the class.

Student Book page 72

10 Communication task:
Would you like to…?

Activity A

1. Have students read the directions for the activity.

2. Focus students' attention on the photos of people doing various activities. Have students identify what is happening in each one (*go to the movies, work out at a gym, play tennis, shop, eat / eat out / eat in a restaurant, sit on the beach, visit a museum, watch / go to a basketball game*).

3. Focus students' attention on the sample conversation. Model it with two students.

4. Explain to students that they will circulate and invite other students to do various activities. Then they will fill in the weekly planner with the students' names and activities. Make sure they understand that they must have a different student and activity per day. Also, make sure they understand that if they have already accepted an invitation for something on a particular day, and another student asks them to do something on the same day, they must say no and give the reason they can't go.

5. *Class activity*. Have students do the activity. Circulate and help as needed.

Extra

Put students in pairs and have them tell their partner about their plans for the week.

Extension

Have one student say what he or she will do on Monday. Have another student say what he or she will do on Tuesday and what the first student will do on Monday. Then have a third student say what he or she will do on Wednesday, what the second student will do on Tuesday, and what the first student will do on Monday. Continue until the seventh student has said what he or she will do on Sunday and what the rest of the students will do. Do the activity again with different students.

Student Book page 88

Check your English

To review the vocabulary and grammar from Unit 12, have students do page 88 in class. This page can be done individually, in pairs, or as a class. It can also be assigned for homework. Alternatively, administer this page as a test at the end of the unit.

Answers:

A Vocabulary
1. going to class
2. going to bed early
3. doing homework
4. taking an exam
5. cleaning the apartment
6. doing the laundry
7. fixing a bicycle
8. baby-sitting

B Grammar
Conversation A
A: Could
B: Do
A: her
B: she
A: it
Conversation B
A: want
B: like / have to
A: would
B: I'd love

Optional activities teaching notes

Optional activity 1.1

Sentence scramble, *page 89*

Preparation: Make one copy of Optional activity 1.1, which consists of two sets of different scrambled sentences, for each pair of students. Cut the copies to separate the two parts.

Procedure: Put students in pairs. Distribute part **A** to one student in each pair and part **B** to the other student in each pair. Have students read the instructions for the activity. Check that students understand the two stages to this activity: First, students unscramble their own sentences. Students can do this individually, and the first student to finish can help his or her partner unscramble the sentences. Students then make short conversations by matching a question from Student A's sheet with a response from Student B's sheet.

Alternate Procedure: Distribute part **A** to half of the class and part **B** to the other half of the class. Have pairs of **A** students work together to unscramble the questions, and have pairs of **B** students work together to unscramble the responses. Then put students in A/B pairs and have them make short conversations by matching a question from Student A's sheet with a response from Student B's sheet.

Answers:
  1. What's your first name?
  e. My first name is Mike.
  2. What's your last name?
  d. My last name is Chen.
  3. What's his last name?
  c. His last name is Somkid.
  4. What's her first name?
  f. Her first name is Julia.
  5. What's your address?
  g. My address is 86 Main Street.
  6. What's your phone number?
  h. My phone number is 246-555-0138.
  7. What's your apartment number?
  b. My apartment number is 6A.
  8. What's your nickname?
  i. My nickname is Buffy.
  9. What's your e-mail address?
  a. It's melinda@go.net.
10. How do you spell that?
  j. It's G-U-P-T-A.

Additional practice: Have students ask each other the questions from part **A** and answer with their own information.

Optional activity 1.2

What's your name?, *page 90*

Preparation: Make one copy of Optional activity 1.2, which consists of four different role cards, for each group of four students. Cut the copies into four role cards. Be sure to keep sets of cards together.

Procedure: Put students into groups of four. Distribute one set of role cards to each group. Students use the information on the cards to have conversations with the other characters in their group and try to identify who the different characters are. Explain the activity to students. Each student (**A**, **B**, **C**, **D**) pretends to be the person described on his/her card. Students ask each other questions in order to fill in the remaining three names in the chart at the bottom of their card.

Have students read the directions on the cards. Model the conversation on Student A's card with a student volunteer. Give students time to do the activity.

Answers:

Student A
a business person:	Joe
a Canadian:	Joanne
a politician:	Joan
an American:	Joe

Student B
an artist:	Joey
an American:	Joe
a Canadian:	Joanne
a singer:	Joanne

Student C
a singer:	Joanne
an artist:	Joey
a British person:	Joan
an Australian:	Joey

Student D
an Australian:	Joey
a politician:	Joan
a business person:	Joe
an American:	Joe

Optional activity 2.1

Family crossword, *page 91*

Preparation: Make one copy of Optional activity 2.1, which consists of two sets of different crossword puzzles and family trees, for each pair of students. Cut the copies to separate the two parts.

Procedure: Put students in pairs. Distribute part **A** to one student in each pair and part **B** to the other student in each pair. There are two stages to this activity: First, students look at the family trees and identify the relationships of the people shown, i.e., grandmother, grandfather, mother, father, etc. Next, students ask each other questions in order to complete their crossword puzzles.

Direct students' attention to the family trees, and give them time to work out the family relationships depicted. Explain that the numbers next to the people in the family trees relates to the numbered words in the crossword puzzles. Have students read the directions for part 1. Direct A students to look at the crossword puzzle and direct B students to look at the family tree. Model the example conversation with a student volunteer. Explain that Student A will ask questions about the crossword puzzle, and Student B will look at the family tree to answer them. Then have students read the directions for part 2. This time, Student B looks at the crossword puzzle and asks questions, while Student A looks at the family tree in order to answer the questions.

Answers:
Student A's crossword puzzle

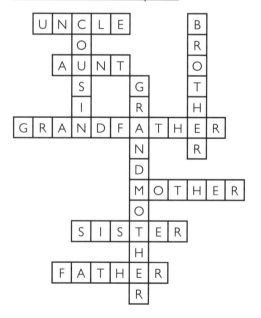

Student B's crossword puzzle

Optional activity 2.2

Concentration, *page 92*

Preparation: Make one copy of Optional activity 2.2 for each group of four students. Cut the handout into cards and keep the set of cards together along with a set of instructions.

Procedure: Divide the class into groups of three or four. Give each group a set of the instructions and cards from the handout. Explain the activity to the class. There are description cards and picture cards. Students will shuffle the two sets of cards and place them face down on the desk or table in two piles. One student in the group will select a picture card and another student in the group will select a description card. That student then reads the description on the card and looks at the picture. The group should ask questions in order to decide if the person pictured matches the description. If the two cards don't match, they are returned to the bottom of the pile, and the next two students in the group select two more cards. Note: There is no one correct answer for many of these cards. Students should use cues such as young, middle-aged, thin, heavy, etc., to help them decide if the description matches the pictures. The aim is to get students discussing and agreeing what these terms mean in relation to the pictures.

Optional activity 3.1

Do you have a bookbag?, *page 93*

Preparation: Make one copy of Optional activity 3.1, which consists of two similar pictures and questions, for each pair of students.

Procedure: Put students into pairs. Distribute part **A** to one student in each pair and part **B** to the other student in each pair. Explain the activity. Students take turns asking each other questions in order to complete their lists. Direct students' attention to the examples in the speech bubbles. Students should ask and answer in full sentences, saying the location of things that they have.

Alternate Procedure: With less confident students, begin the activity by reviewing the items in the checklists to make sure students know what the items are. Then have Student A ask questions for all of the items in his/her checklist first, and have Student B answer. Then have students switch— Student B asks questions to complete his/her checklist while Student A answers.

Additional practice: Have students review their lists and their pictures and compare the differences.

Optional activity 3.2

Electronics questionnaire, *page 94*

Preparation: Make one copy of Optional activity 3.2 for each student.

Procedure: Distribute one copy of the handout to each student. Review the items in the questionnaire to ensure that students understand the vocabulary. Explain the activity to the class. Focus students' attention on the chart. Review the headings and ask students comprehension questions to make sure they understand what to write in each column. For example: *What will you write in the* Comments *column?* Focus students' attention on the example in the chart and the speech bubbles at the bottom of the page. Encourage students to make comments about all of the items, because this will extend the activity and provide students with the opportunity to keep talking.

This can be done as a mixer. Students stand up, walk around, and talk to their classmates. They try to find one person who owns each electronic item. When they find someone who says they own an item, they should write that student's name on the list, then ask if the person likes the item and if they have any comments about it. After students have found someone who has the first item, they should move on and try to find a different person who has the second item, and so on. Alternatively, put students into groups of four or five. Group members should take turns asking one question each, and continuing around the group until the questionnaire is completed.

Optional activity 4.1

Charades, *page 95*

Preparation: Make one copy of Optional activity 4.1 for each group of three or four students. Cut each handout into cards and keep the sets of cards together along with a set of instructions.

Procedure: Divide the class into groups of three or four. Give each group a set of the instructions and cards from the handout. Explain the activity to the class. Ensure that students understand the activity by modeling it with the class. Act out an activity and encourage the class to guess what you are doing. Students arrange the cards face down on the table. They then take turns choosing a card. When students choose a card, they must not show it to the other students in their group. They act out the activity on the card. When their classmates guess the activity correctly, the next student chooses a card and acts out his/her activity.

This game is intended to be a race. When you say *Go!,* all of the groups begin the task. The first group to finish all 15 actions wins.

Optional activity 4.2

Where's Wittaya?, *page 96*

Preparation: Make one copy of Optional activity 4.2, which consists of two similar charts, for each pair of students. Cut the copies to separate the two parts.

Procedure: Put students in pairs. Distribute part **A** to one student in each pair, and part **B** to the other student in each pair. Have students read the instructions for the activity. Model the activity with a student volunteer to ensure that students understand what they should do. Explain the activity to the class. Students take turns asking *Wh-* questions to complete their charts. Although this activity looks very simple, it will require a fair amount of discussion (in English!) for students to complete, because the two charts don't have the information in the same order.

Answers:

City:	Hanoi		City:	Taipei
Person:	Mai		Person:	Hong-yi
Place:	at home		Place:	at home
Activity:	washing dishes		Activity:	taking a shower
City:	Bangkok		City:	São Paulo
Person:	Wittaya		Person:	Mateus
Place:	on a street		Place:	at work
Activity:	eating		Activity:	reading e-mail
City:	New York		City:	Tokyo
Person:	Jill		Person:	Sumio
Place:	at a theater		Place:	at a theater
Activity:	working		Activity:	sleeping
City:	Mexico City		City:	Toronto
Person:	Tomas		Person:	Emma
Place:	at school		Place:	in a store
Activity:	studying		Activity:	playing the piano
City:	London			
Person:	Sally			
Place:	at a party			
Activity:	singing			

Optional activity 5.1

Food questionnaire, *page 97*

Preparation: Make one copy of Optional activity 5.1 for each student.

Procedure: Distribute one copy of the handout to each student. Explain the activity to the class. Focus students' attention on the chart. Review the headings and ask students comprehension questions to make sure they understand what to write in each column. Focus students' attention on the examples in the chart and the example speech bubbles. Encourage students to make comments about the items, because this will extend the activity and provide students with the opportunity to keep talking.

This can be done as a mixer. Students stand up, walk around, and talk to their classmates. They tell their classmates which foods they like and don't like, and find out about their classmates' tastes. They should write down the name of each person they talk to and also write down any comments that are made.

Alternatively, divide the class into groups of three or four and have students complete the questionnaires in groups.

Additional practice: After students have completed the questionnaire, work with the whole class and go around the room asking each student to say one thing that a classmate likes and one thing a classmate dislikes. For example, *Young-soo likes tea. Gabriele doesn't like spaghetti.*

Optional activity 5.2

The snack game, *page 98*

Preparation: Make one copy of Optional activity 5.2 for each pair of students. Cut the word cards to separate them, and keep them with the game board. Each student needs a marker, for example a coin or an eraser, to use as a game piece as well as a coin to flip to decide how many squares to move.

Procedure: Distribute one copy of the handout to each pair of students. Focus students' attention on the game board and elicit the names of the foods and drinks pictured. Explain the activity to the class. Student A flips a coin and moves either one or two squares. Student A then draws a card with a question prompt on it and looks at the picture. Student A uses the prompt card and picture to form a question. For example, with the card that says *Do you eat/drink much/many ...?* + the picture of ice cream, Student A asks Student B *Do you eat much ice cream?* Student B answers the question, then takes a turn. The first student to reach FINISH is the winner. Students should help each other form the questions correctly. You can circulate during the game and listen for correct sentence formation.

Optional activity 6.1

House plans, *page 99*

Preparation: Make one copy of Optional activity 6.1 for each student.

Procedure: Distribute one copy of the handout to each student. Have students read the instructions for the activity. Focus students' attention on the example floor plan. Ask comprehension questions such as, *How many bedrooms does this home have? (Three.) Where is this home? (Near the beach.)* Direct students' attention to the list of home-related vocabulary. Give students time to draw a simple plan for a house. If you like, you can encourage them to draw some of the surrounding area, for example, a beach. If they choose, they can add a helicopter landing pad, airplane runway, music recording studio, or any other special features that you may need to help name. After they have drawn their houses, students talk about their houses with their classmates.

This can be done as a mixer. Students stand up, walk around, and talk to their classmates. They ask about each other's house pictures and explain their own. Alternatively, for a shorter activity, have students work in small groups or pairs.

Additional practice: After students have completed the task, ask them to vote on which house they liked the most.

Optional activity 6.2

Where's the cell phone?, *page 100*

Preparation: Make one copy of Optional activity 6.2, which consists of two sets of similar pictures, for each pair of students. Cut the copies to separate the two parts.

Procedure: Put students in pairs. Distribute part **A** to one student in each pair and part **B** to the other student in each pair. Tell students that they should not look at each other's pictures. Direct students' attention to the small pictures along the side of their handouts. Elicit the names of the items to be sure students have identified them correctly. Explain the activity. First, Student A asks Student B about the five items pictured along the side of the page in part **1**. Student B, whose picture shows where the items are located, answers Student A. Student A draws each item in the correct location. Students switch roles, and Student B asks Student A about the locations of the items shown along the side of his/her handout. At the end, have students compare pictures to check for accuracy.

Optional activity 7.1

What do you do in your free time?, *page 101*

Preparation: Make one copy of Optional activity 7.1 for each student.

Procedure: Put students in pairs. Explain the activity. First, students take turns interviewing one another about their free time activities, noting their partner's response. Then each pair joins with another pair. They take turns explaining their partner's free time activities to the other group members. Finally, students notice whether they share any free time interests with the group.

Focus students' attention on the example speech bubbles. Encourage them to ask their partners follow-up questions about their interests. This will extend the activity and provide students with the opportunity to keep talking.

Optional activity 7.2

How often do you...?, *page 102*

Preparation: Make one copy of Optional activity 7.1 for each group of three students. Cut the picture cards to separate them. Keep them together with a set of instructions and an example questions for groups to use.

Procedure: Divide students into groups of three. Distribute one set cards, instructions, and example questions to each group. Students place the cards with pictures of free time activities face down on the table. Have students read the directions for the activity. Students take turns choosing a card and asking the person on their left at least one appropriate question about the activity shown on the card. Students can use the sample questions and answers to help them as needed. Encourage students to have a short conversation each time, rather than saying simply *yes* or *no*. Model an example conversation with a student volunteer if necessary:

A: Do you like going to the movies?
B: Not really. But I like watching TV.
A: Oh, really? How often do you watch TV?
B: Every day. My favorite show is…

Optional activity 8.1

Are you going to...?, *page 103*

Preparation: Make one copy of Optional activity 8.1 for each student.

Procedure: Distribute one copy of the handout to each student. Explain the activity. First, students work alone to (1) check which life events they think will happen to them and (2) write those events next to a time. Remind students that they can imagine what will happen rather than sharing their own life plans, if they prefer. For more confident classes, elicit ideas of other additional life events and write them on the board for students to use, for example *get married*, *buy a house*, *have children*, *buy a car*, *learn to drive*, etc. Give students time to read through the list of events check their answers, and write them next to a time expression in the chart.

Next put students in pairs. Have them read the directions for part **3**. Following the example conversation, students ask one another about the events in the checklist above, noting when their partner expects each event to happen and sharing as much extra information as possible.

Optional activity 8.2

What are you going to do this weekend?, *page 104*

Preparation: Make one copy of Optional activity 8.2 for each pair of students. Cut the slips apart to separate them. Keep the slips with the schedule.

Procedure: Put students in pairs. Distribute one handout to each pair of students. Have students place the slips face down. Explain the activity. Students take turns choosing a card and filling in the information in the correct place on the schedule. Early finishers can ask one another about their own plans for the weekend.

Answers:

	Friday	Saturday	Sunday
morning		**Activity:** work **Place:** in a restaurant **People:** Mario Mei-ling	**Activity:** go away **Place:** to the beach **People:** Wittaya Kazuo
afternoon		**Activity:** play soccer **Place:** at school **People:** Chul-soo Fadi	**Activity:** visit a museum **Place:** in the city **People:** Hao-yu Adam
evening	**Activity:** dancing **Place:** at a school party **People:** Hiro Becky	**Activity:** see a movie **Place:** at the mall **People:** Hector Simon	**Activity:** study **Place:** at the library **People:** Jason Sam

Optional activity 9.1

Movie madness, *page 105*

Preparation: Make one copy of Optional activity 9.1 for each student.

Procedure: Distribute one copy of the handout to each student. Explain the activity. First, students work alone to complete the movie questionnaire about their own interests. Then they interview one another in pairs and note their partner's responses.

Next students work together to come up with an idea for a movie. This can be very simple, or it can be as wild as students want it to be. Have students share their ideas in small groups or with the whole class.

With less confident classes, elicit movie vocabulary for students to use in both parts of the activity.

Additional practice: To practice the third person form of verbs, have students present the results of the interview from part **1** in small groups or with the whole class.

Optional activity 9.2

Talk show interview, *page 106*

Preparation: Make one copy of Optional activity 9.2 for each student.

Procedure: Distribute one copy of the handout to each student. Explain the activity. Set the scene by reminding students of celebrity interviews on talk shows. Tell them that they are going to interview a partner, taking turns being host and guest. To prepare students for the activity, brainstorm example questions they might ask for each topic given. This is a good opportunity to review a lot of language that students have studied so far. Encourage them to playact the host and celebrity roles as much as possible, and to relax and enjoy the interviews.

Additional practice: Have volunteer pairs perform their interviews for the class.

Optional activity 10.1

I have a headache, *page 107*

Preparation: Make one copy of Optional activity 10.1, which consists of two different crossword puzzles, for each pair of students. Cut the copies to separate the two parts.

Procedure: Put students in pairs. Distribute part **A** to one student in each pair and part **B** to the other student in each pair. Explain the activity. Student A completes his/her crossword by prompting Student B to mime the ailments on Student B's list. Students then switch roles, and Student B asks the questions, while Student A mimes the ailments. Direct students' attention to the example conversation for each part.

After completing the puzzle, Student A will have the word *terrible* running vertically down the middle of the puzzle. Student B will have the words *not so good*.

Answers:

Student A's crossword puzzle

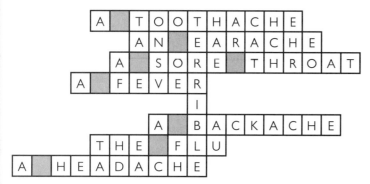

Student B's crossword puzzle

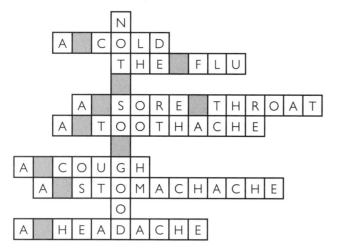

Optional activity 10.2

I have a terrible cold!, *page 108*

Preparation: Make one copy of Optional activity 10.2 for each group of three students. Cut the handout into three sections: Student A, Student B, and Student C. Keep the parts grouped together.

Procedure: Put students in groups of three. Distribute one set of role cards to each group. Have one student in each group take a role card. Explain the activity. On the left side of the role cards, students have some problems that they will ask advice about. Students write the best advice they hear. On the right side of the card, students have advice that they are to give to their classmates. Model a conversation with a volunteer to ensure that students understand the activity.

This can also be done as a mixer. Students stand up, walk around, and tell their classmates what their problems are. They can give the advice on their role card or add advice of their own. Each student should note the advice they like the best for each of their four problems.

Optional activity 11.1

My best vacation ever, *page 109*

Preparation: Make one copy of Optional activity 11.1 for each student.

Procedure: Distribute one handout to each student. Explain the activity. First students unscramble their sentences and then answer the questions. Next students work in pairs, asking one another the questions about their best vacations ever. With a less confident class, have students work in pairs to unscramble the questions. Then elicit ideas for possible answers to the questions. Give students time to do the activity.

Additional practice: After students have completed the task, ask them to form groups of four and to use their notes to tell the group about their partner's best vacation ever.

Optional activity 11.2

My life story, *page 110*

Preparation: Make one copy of Optional activity 11.2 for each student.

Procedure: Distribute one handout to each student. Explain the activity. First students work alone to write information about nine events in their life. They should note what the event was, when it happened, and if possible, add details about how they felt, where they were, and so on. Remind students that these don't have to be important events like moving, they can include anything the student feels like sharing, for example, *Last week, I spent all weekend studying in the library.* Model the activity for the class by presenting examples from your own life and writing them on the board. After all students have completed the chart, put them in pairs and have them ask and answer questions about each other's life story.

Optional activity 12.1

Is Evan there?, *page 111*

Preparation: Make one copy of Optional activity 12.1, which consists of two different sets of cues for phone conversations, for each pair of students. Cut the copies to separate the two parts.

Procedure: First brainstorm telephone language for beginning and ending phone calls, and write it on the board. (*Hello? Is Mike there? Good-bye,* etc.) Put students in pairs. Distribute part **A** to one student in each pair and part **B** to the other student in each pair. Explain the activity. First Student A calls Student B and leaves a message for Student B's roommate Evan. After the call has ended, Student A checks the message for accuracy. Student B then calls Student A to leave a message for Student A's roommate Tonya. Student B then checks Student A's note for accuracy. Finally, both students invent their own activities and meeting places and phone each other again, with another message. This activity can be extended by putting students into different pairs to practice the message they have just made up.

Optional activity 12.2

Would you like to go to a movie?, *page 112*

Preparation: Make one copy of Optional activity 12.1 for each student.

Procedure: Distribute one copy of the handout to each student. Have students read the directions for the activity. Have students choose six items from the list of things they have to do and write them on the calendar. Next have them choose four items from the list of fun activities and write those on the calendar. After they have filled in their calendars, they will have 11 free "slots" to schedule the remaining fun activities with their classmates.

Put students into groups and have them make plans to do things with their classmates. Students write their classmates' names and the activities in the appropriate slot. This can also be done as a mixer. Students stand up, walk around, and ask their classmates to do fun activities with them.

Student A

1. Put the words in order to make questions.

1. your name first What's ? <u>What's your first name?</u>
2. What's name your last ? _____
3. last What's his name ? _____
4. What's name her first ? _____
5. address What's your ? _____
6. number your phone What's ? _____
7. apartment What's number your ? _____
8. nickname What's your ? _____
9. address your What's e-mail ? _____
10. that you How do spell ? _____

2. Have short conversations with Student B. Use the questions above.

A: What's your first name?
B: My first name is Mike.

✂ ---

Student B

1. Put the words in order to make sentences.

a. melinda@go.net It's . <u>It's melinda@go.net.</u>
b. number My 6A apartment is . _____
c. Somkid name His last is . _____
d. Chen name My last is . _____
e. is My Mike first name . _____
f. name Her Julia first is . _____
g. 86 My address Street is Main . _____
h. 246-555-0138 number My phone is . _____
i. My Buffy nickname is . _____
j. G-U-P-T-A It's . _____

2. Answer Student A's questions. Use the sentences above.

A: What's your e-mail address?
B: It's melinda@go.net.

Student A
You are: Name: Joey
              Job: artist
              Nationality: Australian

Talk to Students B, C, and D. Have short conversations. For example:

A: Hi, I'm Joey. What's your name?
B: I'm Joan.
A: Nice to meet you, Joan. Where are you from?
B: I'm from Britain. I'm a politician. How about you? Are you Canadian?
A: No, I'm Australian. I'm an artist.

Find:	Name:
a business person	
a Canadian	
a politician	Joan
an American	

Student B
You are: Name: Joan
              Job: politician
              Nationality: British

Talk to Students A, C, and D. Have short conversations. For example:

A: Hi, I'm Joan. What's your name?
B: I'm Joe.
A: Nice to meet you, Joe. Where are you from?
B: I'm from America. I'm a business person. How about you? Are you Canadian?
A: No, I'm British. I'm a politician.

Find:	Name:
an artist	
an American	Joe
a Canadian	
a singer	

Student C
You are: Name: Joe
              Job: business person
              Nationality: American

Talk to Students A, B, and D. Have short conversations. For example:

C: Hi, I'm Joe. What's your name?
D: I'm Joanne.
C: Nice to meet you, Joanne. Where are you from?
D: I'm from Canada. I'm a singer. How about you? Are you Canadian?
C: No, I'm American. I'm a business person.

Find:	Name:
a singer	Joanne
an artist	
a British person	
an Australian	

Student D
You are: Name: Joanne
              Job: singer
              Nationality: Canadian

Talk to Students A, B, and C. Have short conversations. For example:

D: Hi, I'm Joanne. What's your name?
A: I'm Joey.
D: Nice to meet you, Joey. Where are you from?
A: I'm from Australia. I'm an artist. How about you? Are you American?
D: No, I'm Canadian. I'm a singer.

Find:	Name:
an Australian	Joey
a politician	
a business person	
an American	

Student A

1. Ask Student B questions to complete the crossword puzzle.

Example:
A: Who is number 2?
B: He's my cousin.

2. Look at the picture. Answer Student B's questions.

Example:
B: Who is number 8?
A: He's my grandfather.

✂ -

Student B

1. Look at the picture. Answer Student A's questions.

Example:
A: Who is number 2?
B: He's my cousin.

2. Ask Student A questions to complete the crossword puzzle.

Example:
B: Who is number 8?
A: He's my grandfather.

Instructions

1. Make two sets of cards: (1) pictures and (2) words.
   Put them face down on the table. Make two piles.
2. One person takes a picture card. One person takes a word card.
3. Does the picture match the words? Ask questions.
   Yes = keep your card.   No = put your card back.
4. Play until all the cards are chosen. The winner has the most cards at the end.

Good-looking Japanese man Height: tall Weight: thin Hair: straight, short, dark Age: in his 20s	**Pretty Mexican woman** Height: average Weight: average Hair: long, curly, dark Age: in her 20s	
Handsome Australian man Height: average Weight: average Hair: short, straight, dark Age: in his 70s	**Beautiful Korean woman** Height: short Weight: heavy Hair: long, straight, dark Age: in her 60s	
Pretty American woman Height: average Weight: average Hair: short, curly, blond Age: in her 40s	**Handsome Canadian man** Height: tall Weight: heavy Hair: long, curly, dark Age: in his 30s	
Beautiful Chinese woman Height: short Weight: heavy Hair: long, straight, dark Age: in her 20s	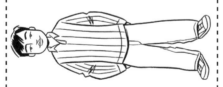	
Good-looking Brazilian man Height: tall Weight: thin Hair: curly, short, dark Age: in his 50s		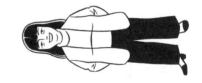
Handsome British man Height: average Weight: average Hair: short, curly, dark Age: in his 30s		

Student A

1. Ask about Student B's picture.	No, I don't have a book.	2. Look at the picture. Answer Student B's questions.
Do you have... ?	**Where is it?**	
❑ a bookbag	*It's on the chair.*	
❑ a ruler		
❑ a book		
❑ a board		
❑ a notebook		
❑ a map		
❑ an electronic dictionary		
❑ an eraser		
❑ a clock		
❑ a pen		
❑ a pencil		
❑ a bulletin board		
❑ a wastebasket		

Yes, I have a bookbag. It's on the chair.

Student B

1. Ask about Student A's picture.	No, I don't have an eraser.	2. Look at the picture. Answer Student A's questions.
Do you have... ?	**Where is it?**	
❑ a bookbag	*It's on the chair.*	
❑ a ruler		
❑ a book		
❑ a board		
❑ a notebook		
❑ a map		
❑ an electronic dictionary		
❑ an eraser		
❑ a clock		
❑ a pen		
❑ a pencil		
❑ a bulletin board		
❑ a wastebasket		

Yes, I have a bookbag. It's on the chair.

Optional activity 3.2   Electronics questionnaire

Ask your classmates about electronics. Complete the questionnaire.

Do you have... ?	What's your name?	Do you like it?			Do you have any comments?
a laptop	Isara	☐ yes	☐ so-so	☑ no	It isn't very good.
an MP3 player		☐ yes	☐ so-so	☐ no	
a CD player		☐ yes	☐ so-so	☐ no	
a television		☐ yes	☐ so-so	☐ no	
a digital camera		☐ yes	☐ so-so	☐ no	
a karaoke machine		☐ yes	☐ so-so	☐ no	
headphones		☐ yes	☐ so-so	☐ no	
a cell phone		☐ yes	☐ so-so	☐ no	
a DVD player		☐ yes	☐ so-so	☐ no	
a camcorder		☐ yes	☐ so-so	☐ no	
a video game system		☐ yes	☐ so-so	☐ no	
a boom box		☐ yes	☐ so-so	☐ no	

It takes good pictures.

It's expensive.

The sound is great!

The screen is too small.

It isn't very good.

Instructions
1. Put the cards face down on the table.
2. Take a card.
3. Act out the word for your partner. No talking! Your partner guesses the word.
4. Take turns until all the cards are chosen.

sleeping	eating lunch	studying
drinking	driving	cooking dinner
going to work	talking on the phone	playing the piano
reading e-mail	shopping	washing dishes
singing	exercising	taking a shower

Student A

Who's studying?

Tomas is.

Ask and answer questions with Student B and complete the chart. Take turns.

City: _____ Person: _____ Place: at home Activity: washing dishes	City: Taipei Person: _____ Place: at home Activity: taking a shower	City: _____ Person: Wittaya Place: _____ Activity: eating
City: São Paolo Person: Mateus Place: _____ Activity: _____	City: _____ Person: Jill Place: _____ Activity: working	City: Tokyo Person: Sumio Place: at a theater Activity: _____
City: Mexico City Person: _____ Place: at school Activity: studying	City: _____ Person: Emma Place: _____ Activity: playing the piano	City: London Person: _____ Place: at a party Activity: singing

What's Sumio doing? He's sleeping. Where's Wittaya? He's on a street in Bangkok.

✄ -

Who's studying?

Tomas is.

Student B

Ask and answer questions with Student A and complete the chart. Take turns.

City: Toronto Person: Emma Place: in a store Activity: _____	City: _____ Person: Tomas Place: _____ Activity: studying	City: Bangkok Person: _____ Place: on a street Activity: eating
City: _____ Person: Sally Place: _____ Activity: singing	City: New York Person: Jill Place: at a theater Activity: _____	City: _____ Person: Sumio Place: _____ Activity: sleeping
City: Hanoi Person: Mai Place: at home Activity: _____	City: _____ Person: Hong-yi Place: _____ Activity: taking a shower	City: _____ Person: Mateus Place: at work Activity: reading e-mail

What's Sumio doing? He's sleeping. Where's Wittaya? He's on a street in Bangkok.

1. Write the English name of five foods or drinks that you like. Write the English name of six foods or drinks that you don't like.
2. Ask your classmates about them. Complete the questionnaire.

I like...	Do you?	What's your name?	Do you have any comments?
1 *steak*	☑ yes ☐ no	Young-Soo	There's a good steak restaurant near my house.
2	☐ yes ☐ no		
3	☐ yes ☐ no		
4	☐ yes ☐ no		
5	☐ yes ☐ no		
6	☐ yes ☐ no		
I don't like...			
7	☐ yes ☐ no		
8	☐ yes ☐ no		
9	☐ yes ☐ no		
10	☐ yes ☐ no		
11	☐ yes ☐ no		
12	☐ yes ☐ no		

I like steak. Do you?

No, I don't.

Yes, I do, too. There's a good steak restaurant near my house.

I don't like tomatoes.

I don't, either.

Oh, really? I do. But I don't like carrots!

1. Draw a simple plan for a house. It can be your real house, or it can be your dream house. It can have a lot of rooms, or only a few. Label the parts of the house.

Example:

bedroom	dining room	
bedroom	bathroom	kitchen
bedroom	living room	

Yard

The beach

kitchen
living room
closet
hall
garage
terrace
dining room
bedroom
bathroom
stairs
yard
balcony

2. Talk to your classmates. Ask and answer questions about your pictures.

Is there a…?   There are…
Are there any…?   There aren't…
How many…?   There's…
Does it have…?   There isn't…

Optional activity 6.2 Where's the cell phone?

Student A

1. Ask Student B where these things are.
   Draw them in the correct place.

2. Look at the picture.
   Answer Student B's questions.

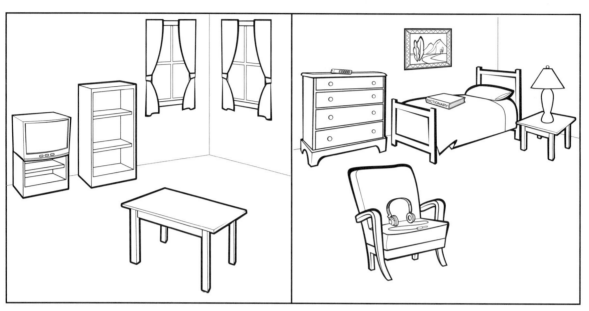

Where is… ?   **Where are… ?**

Student B

1. Look at the picture.
   Answer Student A's questions.

2. Ask Student A where these things are.
   Draw them in the correct place.

Optional activity 7.1   What do you do in your free time?

1. Interview your partner. Ask about free time activities. Make short notes of the answers. Find out about three (or more) free time activities.

Notes

Example: Miguel—listening to music, every night, at home (+ brother)

_____

_____

_____

_____

2. *Group work.* Get together with another pair. Look at your notes. Tell the other pair about your partner.

Example:
Miguel likes listening to music. He listens to music every night at home, with his brother. His favorite bands are… . He doesn't like shopping, but he likes eating out. His favorite restaurants are… .

3. In your group of four, answer the questions.

1. Is there a free-time activity that only one person in the group does? What is it?

2. Is there a free-time activity that more than one person in the group does? What is it?

Optional activity 7.2   How often do you... ?

Instructions

1. Put the cards face down on the table.
2. Take a card.
3. Ask your partner a question about the card using a question from the Person A column.
   Your partner answers with a statement from the Person B column.
4. Take turns until all the cards are chosen.

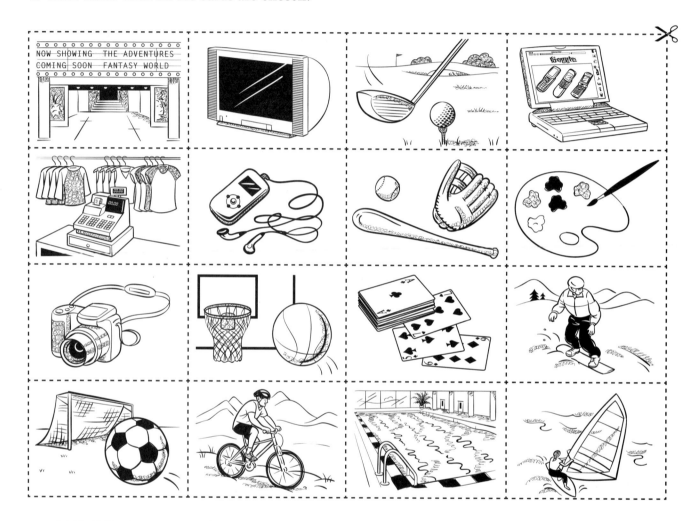

Person A	Person B
___ Can you play/do... ?	___ Yes, I can.
___ Do you like playing/doing/	___ No, I can't.
watching... ?	___ Yes, I do.
___ Me, too!	___ No, I don't.
___ Me neither.	___ Every day.
___ How often do you play/watch/	___ Once a week.
go... ?	___ Twice a week.
___ Where do you... ?	___ Once a month.
___ Who do you ... with?	___ Never.

102   Optional activity 7.2

© Oxford University Press. Photocopiable.

1. Check the events that are going to happen to you. (You can pretend!)

❏ graduate   ❏ go to college   ❏ rent an apartment   ❏ get a job
❏ fall in love   ❏ move   ❏ celebrate a birthday   ❏ travel
❏ take a vacation   ❏ study English   ❏ date a girlfriend or boyfriend

2. Write the events you checked next to a time.

	You	**Your partner**
later today		
tonight		
tomorrow morning		
tomorrow		
this week		
in a few days		
next Sunday		
next weekend		
soon		
next week		
next month		
in a few months		
next year		
in a few years		
in about 5 years		
in about 10 years		
in about 25 years		
someday		

3. Talk with a partner. Ask and answer questions. Share as much information as possible.
Write your partner's events when they say they will happen.

Example:
A: Are you going to go to college?
B: Yes, I am.
A: Great! When are you going?
B: Next year.
A: And where are you going?
B: To Los Angeles.
A: Wow! That's great!
B: What about you? Are you going to college?

Optional activity 8.2 What are you going to do this weekend?

Friday	Saturday	Sunday	
Instructions • Take turns. • Take a card. Read it. • Write the information on the schedule. • Play until the table is filled in.	Activity: _____ Place: _____ People: _Mario_	Activity: _____ Place: _____ People: _Wittaya_	morning
	Activity: _____ Place: _____ People: _Chul-soo_	Activity: _____ Place: _____ People: _Hao-yu_	afternoon
Activity: _____ Place: _At a school party_ People: _____	Activity: _see a movie_ Place: _____ People: _____	Activity: _study_ Place: _____ People: _Jason_	evening

✂

Jason: I'm going to go to the library.

Sam: I'm going to study.

Adam: I'm going to do something with Hao-yu in the city.

Chul-soo: I'm going to be at school!

Hao-yu: I'm going to visit a museum.

Wittaya: I'm going to go away.

Mei-Ling: I'm going to work with Mario.

Becky: I'm going to go dancing with Hiro.

Mario: I'm going to do something in a restaurant on Saturday morning.

Kazuo: On Sunday morning, I'm going to be at the beach.

Fadi: I'm going to play soccer with Chul-soo.

Hiro: I'm going to do something on Friday night.

Hector: I'm going to see a movie.

Simon: I'm going to be at the mall on Saturday night.

104 Optional activity 8.2

© Oxford University Press. Photocopiable.

1. Movie questionnaire

Write about yourself. Then ask your partner and write the answers.

> What's your favorite movie/actor/actress?

> What kind of movies do/don't you like?

> How often do you go to the movies?

	Me	My partner
Name:		
Likes:		
Doesn't like:		
Goes to movies (how often):		
Favorite movie		
Favorite actor:		
Favorite actress:		

2. Create a movie

Example:

What kind of movie is it (action, comedy, etc.)? Action
Who's in the movie (you can choose any actors or actresses, alive or dead)? Audrey Hepburn and Bruce Lee
Where does it happen? In Hong Kong
What happens in the movie? Bruce Lee is in danger. Audrey Hepburn saves him. They get married.
What's the name of the movie? "Jail Bird"

Work with your partner. Create an idea for a movie.

What kind of movie is it (action, comedy, etc.)?
Who's in the movie (you can choose any actors or actresses, alive or dead)?
Where does it happen?
What happens in the movie?
What's the name of the movie?

Interview your partner. Ask at least one question about each topic 1–7.
Think of one more topic to ask about. Then change roles.

Questions
Do you ever… ?
How often do you… ?
What's your favorite… ?

Topics
1. food
2. movies
3. sports
4. TV shows
5. music
6. books, magazines, newspapers
7. free time activities
8. your idea: _____

Answers
I … a lot.
I always…
I usually…
I often…
I sometimes…
I hardly ever…
I never…
I love…
I like…
… is/are OK
I don't really like…
I can't stand…
My favorite … is…

What about movies? What's your favorite movie?

My favorite movie is *Star Wars*.

Do you ever eat fish?

I eat fish a lot!

How often do you eat fish?

I eat fish every day.

OK. And how often do you go to the movies?

Oh, I go…

Student A

1. Ask Student B questions to complete the puzzle. Find the hidden word.

2. Answer Student B's questions by acting out the health problem. Don't speak!

A: Number 1. How do you feel?
B: (Acts out a toothache.)

1. a cold
2. the flu
3. a sore throat
4. a toothache
5. a cough
6. a stomachache
7. a headache

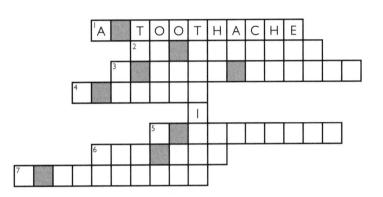

Hidden word:
How do you feel?

I feel _____!

Student B

1. Answer Student A's questions by acting out the health problem. Don't speak!

B: Number 1. How do you feel?
A: (Acts out a cold.)

1. a toothache
2. an earache
3. a sore throat
4. a fever
5. a backache
6. the flu
7. a headache

2. Ask Student A questions to complete the puzzle. Find the hidden words.

Hidden words:
How do you feel?

I feel _____!

Optional activity 10.2   I have a terrible cold!

Student A

Tell your classmates your problems. Write the best advice you hear.

I have a terrible…   I'm really…

backache _____

headache _____

stomachache _____

tired _____

Good idea! Thanks!
Thanks, but I don't think that will help.

Give advice to your classmates.

You should take / see / stay in / drink…

some cough syrup

a dentist

bed

lots of water

your idea _____

Student B

Tell your classmates your problems. Write the best advice you hear.

I have a terrible…   I think I have…

earache _____

cold _____

sore throat _____

a fever _____

Good idea! Thanks!
Thanks, but I don't think that will help.

Give advice to your classmates.

You should drink / stay
You shouldn't eat…

desserts

some tea

home and relax

exercise

your idea _____

Student C

Tell your classmates your problems. Write the best advice you hear.

I have a terrible…   I think I have…
I get a lot of…

cough _____

toothache _____

the flu _____

colds _____

Good idea! Thanks!
Thanks, but I don't think that will help.

Give advice to your classmates.

You should take / go / stay in / drink
You shouldn't…

some aspirin

to bed early

a hot bath

work too hard

your idea _____

1. Put the words in order to make questions.

1. did you where go ? _Where did you go?_____
2. go did when you ? _____
3. long stay did you how ? _____
4. do you did what ? _____
5. you see what did ? _____
6. visit what you did ? _____
7. have you did any problems ? _____
8. go you with who did ? _____
9. most the enjoy what did you ? _____
10. food what eat kind did of you ? _____
11. buy souvenirs did you kind what ? _____
12. people any did meet you ? _____
13. good any photos take you did ? _____
14. feel when home came did you how ? _____

2. Answer the questions about your best vacation ever. Then ask a partner and note the answers.

	Me	My partner
1.		
2.		
3.		
4.		
5.		
6.		
7.		
8.		
9.		
10.		
11.		
12.		
13.		
14.		

Optional activity 11.2 My life story

1. Think of nine events (big or small) in your life. Write about them in order. Say when they happened. Add extra information if you can.

I was born…	My family moved…	I grew up…	I started school…	I attended high school…
I graduated…	I took a trip to…	I entered college…	I visited…	I met…
when I was five	*ten years ago*	*last year*	*last month*	*last week*

Example:
1. *I was born in Bangkok in 1990. My father was working there.*
2. *My family moved to Chiang Mai when I was two. I can't remember living in Bangkok, but I remember Chiang Mai.* And so on.

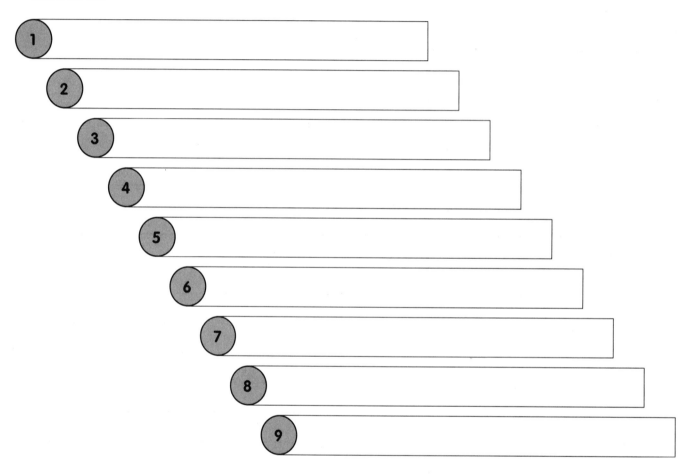

2. Work with a partner. Talk about your life. Ask and answer questions.

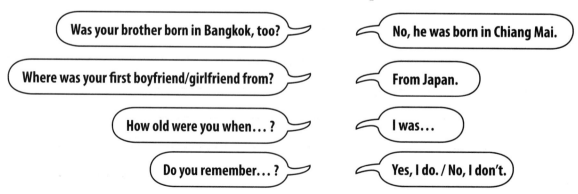

Was your brother born in Bangkok, too? — No, he was born in Chiang Mai.

Where was your first boyfriend/girlfriend from? — From Japan.

How old were you when…? — I was…

Do you remember…? — Yes, I do. / No, I don't.

Student A

1. You want to meet Evan at the library on Friday night.

1. Call Evan's house.

2. Ask to speak to Evan.

3. Leave a message. Say

   • your name.
   • your telephone number.
   • that you want to meet Evan at the library at 8:00 on Friday night to study.
   • that you want Evan to call you back.
   • thank you and good-bye.

B: *Hello?*
A: *Hello, is Evan there?*
B: *Who's calling, please?*
A: *This is…*

2. When you finish, check the message Student B wrote. Is all of the information correct?

3. Your roommate is Tonya. Tonya isn't home right now. The phone rings. Answer it.

1. Say hello.

2. Find out who's calling.

3. Ask if they want to leave a message. If yes, take the message. Write it here.

4. When you finish, show the message to Student B. Is the message correct?

5. Now think of a different plan you'd like to make with Evan. Call his house again. Leave another message.

6. Student B will call you again with another message for Tonya. Take the message.

Student B

1. Your roommate is Evan. Evan isn't home right now. The phone rings. Answer it.

1. Answer the phone.

2. Find out who's calling.

3. Ask if they want to leave a message. If yes, take the message. Write it here.

B: *Hello?*
A: *Hello, is Evan there?*
B: *Who's calling, please?*
A: *This is…*

2. When you finish, show the message to Student A. Is all of the information correct?

3. You want to meet Tonya at the cafe on Wednesday afternoon.

1. Call Tonya's house.

2. Ask to speak to Tonya.

3. Leave a message. Say:

   • your name.
   • your telephone number.
   • that you want to meet Tonya at the cafe at 1:00 on Wednesday afternoon to eat lunch.
   • that you want Tonya to call you back.
   • thank you and good-bye.

4. When you finish, check the message Student A wrote. Is the message correct?

5. Student A will call you again with another message for Evan. Take the message.

6. Now think of a different plan you'd like to make with Tonya. Call her house again. Leave another message.

1. These are things you have to do this week. Choose six. Check them.
   Decide when you are going to do them. Write them in the calendar.

☐ take an exam   ☐ clean the apartment   ☐ go to the dentist   ☐ *your idea* _____

☐ do the laundry   ☐ fix a bicycle   ☐ go shopping for food   ☐ *your idea* _____

☐ baby-sit   ☐ do your homework   ☐ go to class

2. These are things you want to do for fun this week. Choose four. Check them.
   Decide when you are going to do them. Write them in the calendar.

☐ play tennis   ☐ see a movie   ☐ go to a concert   ☐ go to a soccer game   ☐ *your idea* _____

☐ meet friends   ☐ visit a museum   ☐ go shopping for clothes   ☐ go to a museum   ☐ *your idea* _____

	Monday	Tuesday	Wednesday	Thursday	Friday	Saturday	Sunday
Morning							
Afternoon							
Evening							

3. Now talk to your classmates. Invite them to do the six things you *didn't* check, above.
   Choose times when you are both free. Write the plan in the calendar.

> I'm sorry, I can't. I have to…

> Would you like to go to a concert on Friday night?

> Sure, I'd love to! What time?

